PUTTING THE
HUM♥N
BACK INTO
HR

Success as an HR professional
begins with **you**

SU PATEL

RETHINK PRESS

First published in Great Britain 2018
by Rethink Press (www.rethinkpress.com)

*This book is dedicated to my daughter, Pia,
who is my inspiration. My life began after
you came into my world, my angel.*

First my daughter; forever my friend.

Praise

'An organisation's success depends on its people and the leaders' ability to create an environment that brings out the best in every employee. In a world of personalisation, one approach will not suffice! Instead, leaders must work even harder to deeply get to know each employee and their unique attributes. This book does an exceptional job of bringing back the accountability, responsibility and honour of leadership to our consciousness. Importantly, it provides HR practitioners with pragmatic tools to translate this learning into measurable, behavioural change to support and accelerate business performance.'
   — Denise Peart
   Global HR Executive

'A great read, which I would highly recommend not only for HR professionals, but for those who want to understand how a business can do better by its people. This book has reminded me why I became an HR professional and why I love what I do. Su has provided us all with an amazing take on how we can all achieve the best not only for our employees but for our organisations too. I couldn't agree more with her approach and thoughts throughout this. My new career bible sorted.'
   — Danni Cripps
   HR Manager

'This book is a revelation in so many ways! For me, it reminded me that HR isn't complicated. Of course complications arise; that's never going to stop. But when businesses – more specifically, HR – lose sight of people, whether those people are your customers or your employees, is when the biggest complications manifest and take over. This book reminded me that putting people first has to be the foundation of any HR practitioner – It just makes sense!'
   — **Martin Brimicombe**
      Head of HR

'Wow, what a refreshing view of HR. I wish I'd had this support guide when I started my HR career. It would have saved me a lot of frustration and often feeling that I wasn't making a difference! Su has written a guidebook that is brilliantly simple to understand and beautifully practical for anyone in an HR role. I would also encourage anyone leading people to read this too. Having a growth mindset, and focusing on being in the service of people, eradicates the corrosive and often inhuman ego-fuelled HR leadership. Well done for a wonderful book.'
   — **Sarah Francis**
      Owner and Director of
      Every Cloud Coaching Ltd

'*Putting The Human Back Into HR* is a refreshing exploration into the 'brand' of HR. Su is a natural storyteller who uses real and practical experiences over the course of her successful career to showcase her unique perspective on what it truly means to be an HR leader, with making a difference to people being the essence of every chapter. This book will guide curious minds to explore some of the simplest tactics to achieve success as an HR practitioner and the HR Brand Blueprint demonstrates this perfectly. Insightful, honest and reflective throughout, Su guides the reader through a range of topics designed to provoke thought and action to fully connect with people on every level.'

— **Sian Evans**
Senior People Business Partner

Contents

Foreword

Ever heard the phrase 'People leave managers, not companies'? There's definitely some truth in it, and I say that both from personal experience and from more than seventeen years of experience working in recruitment. This statement is especially pertinent to organisations that employ such managers. Does the manager in question have the right resources available to them to ensure their management skills are great?

Having spent most of my working years in the recruitment industry, I have established some amazing and long-lasting relationships with HR managers across different companies, both small to medium-sized enterprises (SMEs) and large corporates. At the same time, I have experienced challenging times and uphill struggles while attempting to form great working partnerships with HR managers.

Why is this? After all, aren't we all aiming for the same thing: to find amazing talent to nurture and nourish to grow the business? Unfortunately, although many HR managers want to focus on employees and creating an inspiring culture, they are inundated with policies, processes and paperwork. All this causes them stress and leads them to missing out on creating great working relationships, both externally and internally.

HR has become an unnecessary evil to many standing on the outside looking in. Hiring managers and candidates alike feel that HR is always in their way, when all HR is doing is finding its own way.

It is a real honour to write this foreword for Su Patel, the founder of HR Training and Consulting Ltd. As Su so rightly says, human resources has the word 'human' in it, yet the human element can so easily be forgotten. Su's system and methodology bring humanity back to the forefront, which allows HR professionals to be seen as humans again.

I first met Su Patel in 2016, and what impressed me most about her was how she applied her knowledge. HR requires people, personal development and, of course, policies and processes. Su brings all these elements together when she works with her clients and balances them in a way I have rarely witnessed, enabling businesses to be both efficient and engaging. Her passion for the HR industry is second to none.

Any industry, especially one overseen by governing bodies like the Chartered Institute of Personnel and Development and the Recruitment and Employment Confederation, can be reluctant to change procedures, even those that are outdated and need to be refreshed. People may realise that their industry needs to change, but they continue to talk about it without taking action. It takes a different type of professional to challenge the status quo: a person who really wants to be a trailblazer for change, a person who won't accept things as they are – especially when they no longer work, a person who cares for the people working in an organisation and can recognise potential when others can't, a person who will speak up and stand out.

That person is undoubtedly Su Patel. With her proven system, the HR Brand Blueprint, Su is destined to make a mark in the industry permanently. For every HR professional out there, this system will be a game-changer. For every small business that needs an external HR professional, Su Patel is the perfect fit. She'll bring people and profit together without compromising on either. The HR industry will be looking to Su Patel for years to come and will learn a lot from her expertise. I urge every HR professional to use this book as their bible. I certainly have no hesitation in associating my brand with hers and have complete faith in her success.

Thanks again, Su, for inviting me to write this foreword and I wish you every success with your book.

— **Deenita Pattni**
Speaker, mentor and award-winning author of *Recruitment Gems Uncovered* and *Pay It Forward: Notes to My Younger Self*, founder of Viamii Training Academy, www.viamii.com

My story

Do you feel like you have a gift? Not just any gift, but a gift nobody fully appreciates?

Let me take you back to 2016. It's a blustery March morning in a training centre. The wind is rattling through the closed windows; the walls are bare; the room is cold and uninspiring. It is sparsely furnished with a desk and some chairs, and contains two people: a man – let's call him Jack – and me.

'Su,' Jack says, 'I'm sorry to say that you didn't pass the interview. You came across as an individual who doesn't really understand the role of an HR manager, and we feel that you will over-promise and under-deliver.'

I am immediately confused.

'How can you say that, Jack? Just last week, you told me in my review that I had delivered outstanding re- sults compared to the rest of the group, and exceeded your expectations. You said that the store managers felt supported, and that I helped improve the culture in some of our shops.'

Jack shifts awkwardly in his seat.

'I'm sorry, Su, you didn't pass the interview, and now we need to discuss your options. You can either apply for a secondment, or pick the option of redundancy…'

'Redundancy, Jack? But I've been doing this for twenty years.'

Back then, I felt exactly like a rug had been pulled out from under my feet. I honestly couldn't understand what I was hearing. Throughout my long-standing career, managers had frequently introduced me as Su Patel, the best HR manager they had ever worked with. One who made a difference. One who made col- leagues feel valued.

As I sat in that cold and uninspiring room with Jack, twenty years rolled away. Suddenly, I was back on the shop floor early one Monday morning in 1996. My job title was operations manager, and I was busy building a cereal display with a young He-Man look-alike. We'll call him Dave.

'The display looks awesome, Dave,' I said. 'Thanks for your help. You're always making things happen – so, what are your plans? What do you want to do next?'

'Thanks, Su. Between you and me, I'm looking for management roles in other companies.'

This confused me – Dave was one of our firm's rising stars. I only had to spend a few moments with him to realise that he was going places.

'Why are you looking for jobs in other companies? Couldn't you be a manager here?'

'I've tried, Su. I've spoken to the HR manager, but nobody's interested. They're always too busy to listen, and they recruit managers from outside, anyway.'

'I'm really disappointed to hear that. Why don't we catch up over coffee later after my walk round?'

I began my morning inspection to make sure everything in the shop was as it should be. I wanted the store manager – let's just call him the boss – to be especially happy with the standards today.

The boss walked in wearing his trademark suit and red tie.

'Morning, boss. How are you?' I got a grunt in reply. 'Ready for the walk round? We've been working hard over the weekend and the store is looking great!'

'Oh, really?' said the boss, dismissively. 'Where's Mike? Has he been working overnight? Oh, there he is… Mike, what on earth do you look like? Look at the state of you! You haven't shaved or tucked in your shirt; you look like you just stepped out of a skip!'

I winced. It was clear that poor Mike was completely shattered after his fourteen-hour shift.

We passed aisle one – there was a mess on the floor. Aisle two's tins weren't stacked exactly like a neat row of soldiers.

'What is that?'

'What do you mean, boss?'

'There! There's a price label missing.'

'I'll get it sorted out as soon as we've finished the walk round…'

'No, you're not listening! Why is it missing and who is responsible? Is it you, Mike, or is it you, Su? Come on, are you fucking stupid? What kind of standards do you have here?'

Have you ever known that someone is treating you in a completely unacceptable way – so much so that you're too shocked to react? This was the day I realised that not only was it unacceptable for managers to speak to their people like that, but it was also unacceptable for people with potential to be carelessly brushed aside. It was then that I decided I was going to make a difference. Something would have to change.

And so, that very night found me with my bible... only this wasn't the story of God. It was the Dale Carnegie bible, entitled *How to Win Friends and Influence People*. The book was a revelation.

'It says here that the number one thing people need, after food and shelter, is to feel important. But no one feels important in our place of work.'

There it was: the difference I wanted to make. I was going to make sure that everybody felt important.

Just two weeks later, I encountered Kevin. Kevin was high up, always happy and impeccably well-groomed, and he made everybody feel important. But

I had no idea he knew who I was until he asked to speak to me.

'Su, I've been hearing some great feedback about you over the last few months. We can't keep you in this role for ever, so what do you really want to do?'

'I'd really like to get into personnel… or HR, I think it's called now.'

Kevin nodded his approval. 'OK – just leave it to me.'

Have you heard the saying 'be careful what you wish for'? I went from being an operations manager in one store on the Friday to being an HR manager in another on the Monday. The smell of freshly-baked bread and the beeping of the industrial cleaning machine made me feel like I was on familiar ground, and I also noticed that people were still not feeling very important.

'Hello, I'm Su, the new HR manager. How are you? How do you like working here?'

My colleagues immediately looked at me with suspicion.

'Why are you asking us that?'

'Well, I just wanted to see how it is for you guys here and get to know how you're feeling.'

'Nobody ever asks us how we're feeling.'

'So, what can we improve, then? How can we make this a better place for you to work in?'

This question received all types of answers, from improved shift rotas to increased stocks of toilet rolls. I certainly had my work cut out for me!

Over the next twenty years, I did all I could to make people feel important, from providing hot food to staff breaking their Ramadan fast, to developing talent across the business, to training over 300 HR managers within the company on how to be. In all, I impacted the lives of over 200,000 employees and really felt like I was making a difference.

That was, until I arrived in the training room with Jack.

I knew that his decision was a done deal. I couldn't change his mind, even though he kept on telling me that he knew I had put my heart and soul into my role, and that it was really about numbers. To be fair, I believe that he was just the messenger. He didn't support what was happening to me, but he couldn't help me, either.

It was time for me to take my talent where it would be appreciated. And so, I listened to the advice of an old colleague.

'You're the person who has made a difference, you're the person who's been helping everybody, so why don't you create your own business so that you can help other people do the same?'

Through this conversation, I realised that this was what I was meant to do next, so I didn't delay. Within two weeks, I'd got a contract with a local school, and through networking, I built a portfolio of clients.

HR Training and Consulting was born.

Now that I was on the outside looking in, I realised that sadly, the picture hadn't changed much since my experience with the boss all those years ago. Managers weren't using talent to its full potential, and people were still being treated like numbers. I met people working in HR and consultants in SMEs who were unsure about what they needed to do. They were detached from the core business and they were struggling to build a relationship with the directors and their teams. I discovered a great deal of self-importance, and very little in the way of making others feel important.

This is why I came up with my HR Brand Blueprint system.

Who is this book for?

What exactly is HR? What does it involve?

I went into HR because I wanted to work with people. Many HR professionals decide on a career in HR because they like working with people, too, but the job often becomes about policies, processes and delivering business results. HR professionals are employed by businesses, so the role is seen as one that supports the business more than the employees. As a result, at times, employees may feel as though they are being treated unfairly.

Unless HR professionals have the key leadership skills to influence and challenge unfair practices, they will struggle to make an impact in their organisation. Above all, they will fail to gain the hearts and minds of the employees who work there. Having said that, there are unfortunately some HR professionals who come across as intimidating and ego driven because 'they know best', causing the organisation's directors to see HR as a restriction rather than a resource.

I wrote this book to help HR professionals realise they are not alone in the challenges that they are facing, and to help them make a bigger impact on their organisations and get the results they want in their careers. I want them to feel valued in the role they perform, confident to take a stand on what's right for people, brave enough to challenge poor practices, and proud of the work they do and what they contribute. I also want to provide them with the tools to play a bigger game.

Are you asking yourself:

- How can I influence change to create a great place for employees to work?

- How can I get my directors/managers to listen to me?

- I am constantly overwhelmed with things to do; what should I focus on?

- Where can I find the answers and the support I need when I need it?

- How can I show the directors the value that HR adds to the business?

- I am often drained from people bringing me bad news; how can I enjoy my job more?

- How can I handle difficult conversations with managers/directors/employees?

- How do I know if I'm doing a great job?

- I love working with people, but I spend most of my time ticking boxes; how can I change that?

- I have completed my HR qualification; how can I apply what I know in the workplace?

- How can I progress my HR career faster?

This book will not give you in-depth knowledge about employment law or policies. There is a vast array of HR books on the theories behind HR management, law, building HR strategy, recruitment and performance. This is not one of those books. Instead, it will give you practical and real-world ideas about how to make HR stand out as a credible brand within your business or organisation.

Professional qualifications will give you the theory and the research, and there are many articles and blogs that will educate you on employee management and managing staff issues, but for me, how to apply these skills in the workplace is what is missing. How can we bring it all together? How can we put our expertise into action at work? What will we focus on? Should everything be about key performance indicators (KPIs) and results, or is it really about listening to the employees? How can we find the right balance as HR professionals?

The methods I describe in this book have helped me to answer these questions, and I hope they will also help you. Therefore, this book is about your personal development. It is about how you can bring all the areas of HR together to feel more fulfilled in your role, bring your team along with you, and ultimately create a strong HR brand within your business or organisation: one that delivers a recognisable service.

In HR, we make relationships the core of what we do. Everything is important: processes, productivity, performance and making progress. But if we don't bridge the gap between the way we work and how we relate to the people within our business or organisation, all of these things are irrelevant, so that is exactly what this book intends to do.

Some truths about HR

Human resources – or personnel management, as it used to be called – has been evolving quickly, but are companies keeping up?

It's been interesting to observe how the profession has evolved over the years, from the times of industrial relations to the current digital advancement period. I recently met with some former colleagues – friends who work for big companies – and from our conversations, I observed that they are living in an HR industry bubble: travelling the world to see the latest technologies that could make their work easier. In comparison, the world of HR in small and medium-sized enterprises (SMEs) often hasn't even left the ground. Many small business owners who take on staff do not even see the importance of a simple handbook or contract, let alone appraisals.

As a consultant, I sometimes find engaging with small business owners a struggle. Some have a preconceived idea that HR is too expensive and will restrict them from doing the things they want to do in their businesses. Let's get started on our journey with a few hard truths about the HR industry. You may recognise some of these from personal experiences.

Truth 1: HR is not at the top of the agenda for some business leaders, who are too busy following their vision, bringing in revenue, minimising costs and maximising profits. This all leaves little time or energy for HR red flags.

Truth 2: HR has seen a lot of negativity over the years. Many managers have lost respect for HR as they believe it puts too many restrictions on a business. Employees have also lost respect for HR for not listening to their needs, leaving them feeling ignored and unimportant.

Truth 3: HR was once viewed as a matronly role: a role that was about staff welfare. It was later described as 'pink and fluffy', becoming the agony aunt for employees. This image neither helps people understand the power of HR, nor supports the growth of a business.

Truth 4: HR has become a box to tick. It's so focused on strategy that the real needs of employees and managers get swept under the carpet.

Truth 5: There is little training available to help HR professionals become more confident in their roles. In the UK, even after they've completed a full Chartered Institute of Personnel and Development (CIPD) qualification, many HR professionals remain unsure about how to apply the theory they've learned within the workplace. A lot of the learning happens on the job, where they have to fit in and do the best they can, but where do they start?

Truth 6: Many HR professionals are not sure of managers' expectations or what employees want from them, depending on which side of the fence they are on. HR often follows the agenda of managers and directors whose priorities focus on making sales and cutting costs as opposed to looking out for the wellbeing of their staff.

Truth 7: HR professionals can become isolated because they are unsure whom to speak to if they encounter problems. Many are judged for not knowing something that may seem simple to others, particularly during their early days in the profession.

Truth 8: HR is a fundamental part of every business that employs staff. It is not just for large companies that can afford a full-time HR department. The key to growing a successful business is getting the right people to do the right things at the right time, and the risk of getting it wrong is too high for small businesses to carry. Employing the right staff will also give business owners more time to work on strategy and strengthening client relationships.

Truth 9: HR's role has evolved to ensure that a partnership develops between staff and managers, which includes finding innovative ways to align the organisation's growth with the growth of employees and leaders within the organisation.

Truth 10: HR needs to become a brand that business owners can be proud of. A brand that provides flexibility and adaptability to each organisation. A brand that impacts an organisation's employees as they grow with the business. A brand that is fresh and balanced. A brand that leads people, yet walks alongside them. A brand that is a courageous, respected and essential function in every business. And I am on a mission to influence the industry to take this on.

If you're ready to create your own HR brand, let's move on.

CHAPTER ONE

HR In The Real World

Since I started working as a consultant, I have pitched my HR services to many business owners. Some get it immediately; others look at me in confusion.

So, what do I actually do? Let's take a look at some definitions of HR.

The business dictionary definition:

'The resource that resides in the knowledge, skills and motivation of people. Human resource is the least mobile of the four factors of production and (under the right conditions) improves with age and experience, which no other resource can do. It is therefore regarded as the scarcest and most crucial productive resource that creates the largest and longest-lasting advantage for any organisation.'

The Chartered Institute of Personnel Development (CIPD) definition:

'HR is about helping an organisation create value through its people – literally providing human resources. The work of an HR professional will vary depending on the type and size of their organisation, but could include recruiting people, training and developing employees, and helping to decide how staff should be paid and rewarded. There are even roles which focus on employment law and protecting the rights of employees at work. HR professionals will also often deal with legal issues, help to shape the culture of their organisations, and focus on what keeps their colleagues productive and engaged.'

My definition is this: HR is about protecting a business as well as being proactive in the way the business looks after its employees. It is about serving the people in a business, meaning the business owners and their employees.

Yes, that's it. Nothing too scary or complicated about it. Yet, HR becomes complicated when we as HR professionals are not sure what we are supposed to be doing.

In my many years of experience, I have worked with several businesses. At an operational level, it's all very simple. HR is about people and how they are treated. But some organisations have moved in the opposite direction when it comes to HR and made it all about strategy. Have you noticed that often when you read about HR, you see constant references to becoming a strategic business partner? But what has this reinvention of the HR role to become more strategic actually achieved?

Unfortunately, it has created a bad reputation for HR professionals. Business owners don't like us, as they feel we restrict them with policies and processes. Meanwhile, employees don't like us because we seem to favour business results rather than show compassion and understanding. I have heard HR referred to as 'human remains'. It amazes me how we say we are all about people, when actually, it appears – at least to outsiders – that we are not. I have witnessed many poorly performing HR professionals in my career. I have even heard of grievances against HR managers.

Some organisations no longer tend to recognise the need for HR, placing full people accountability on line managers. These managers don't always receive appropriate training, though, and are usually more focused on the operational side of the business, which results in lack of development, disengagement, and loss of great talent.

HR has become a joke

Thankfully, there aren't too many HR-based jokes flying around, but there is one particular yarn I want to share with you.

HEAVEN AND HELL

An HR manager was tragically hit by a bus and died. Her soul arrived at the Pearly Gates, where Saint Peter welcomed her.

'Before you get settled in,' he said, 'we have a little problem. You see, we've never had an HR manager make it this far before and we're not really sure what to do with you.'

'Oh, I see,' said the woman. 'Can't you just let me in?'

'Well, I'd like to,' said Saint Peter, 'but I have orders from above. We have been instructed to let you have a day in Hell and a day in Heaven, and then you are to choose where you'd like to go for all of eternity.'

'Actually, I think I'd prefer Heaven,' said the woman.

'Sorry, we have rules...'

Saint Peter put the HR manager into the downward-bound elevator. As the doors opened to Hell, she stepped out on to a beautiful golf course. In the distance was a country club; around her were many friends: past fellow executives, all smartly dressed, happy, and cheering for her. They ran up and kissed her on both cheeks, and they talked about old times.

They played a perfect round of golf, and afterwards, went to the country club where she enjoyed a superb steak and lobster dinner. She met the Devil (who was actually rather nice), and she had a wonderful night telling jokes and dancing.

Before she knew it, it was time to leave. Everyone shook her hand and waved goodbye as she stepped into the elevator. The elevator went back up to Heaven, where Saint Peter was waiting for her.

'Now, it's time to spend a day in Heaven,' he said.

So, she spent the next twenty-four hours lounging around on clouds, playing the harp and singing, which was almost as enjoyable as her day in Hell. At the day's end, Saint Peter returned.

'So,' he said, 'you've spent a day in Hell and you've spent a day in Heaven. Now, you must choose between the two.'

The woman thought for a second and replied, 'Well, Heaven is certainly lovely, but I actually had a better time in Hell. I choose Hell.'

Accordingly, Saint Peter took her to the elevator again and she went back down to Hell. When the elevator opened, she found herself standing in a desolate wasteland covered in garbage and filth. She saw her friends dressed in rags, picking up rubbish and putting it in old sacks. The Devil approached her and put his arm around her.

'I don't understand,' stuttered the HR manager. 'The other day I was here, and there was a golf course, and a country club. We ate lobster, and we danced and had a wonderful, happy time. Now, there's just a dirty wasteland of garbage and all my friends look miserable.'

The Devil simply looked at her and smiled.

'Yesterday, we were recruiting you. Today you're staff.'

Have you finished laughing yet?

The joke has serious points to it – not to mention raising a number of issues about attracting candidates. It questions how we care for our new employees; it questions how we deliver on promises; and it questions trust.

This joke is regularly posted on social media platforms. On LinkedIn recently, it gained over 38,000 likes and a selection of comments, including:

- How true

- Reality it is

- Yes, I've been there. More than once. Moral of the story: candidates are told to be honest while employers repeatedly lie to them

- Haha… yes, I have definitely experienced this

- In real life, HR would put the blame on the employees

- What goes around comes around

- Reality tracks this joke or vice-versa! HR will never change from such practices

- Hahahahaha… that's exactly what is happening in today's organisations

If you work in HR, how does it feel to read comments like these? How can we expect to deliver change, motivate and develop others, or build great cultures within the organisations we work for if this is people's perception of HR in general? The impact of this perception creates further challenges for any HR professionals working at an operational level.

So, what has gone wrong? And how do we fix the problem? Let's take a closer look at some of the challenges we face.

The challenges of HR

Poor HR practices impact on both the individual at a personal level and the company they work for.

Impact of poor HR practices

Personal	Business
Not feeling respected by the people we work with	Great talent leaving the business
Low confidence due to lack of information	Poor employee engagement and culture
Working alone	Lack of leadership development
Struggling to influence at all levels, which results in little buy-in and an inability to drive significant changes	Not achieving the results and targets set by the business
Being afraid to ask for feedback	Negative feedback from customers

How did we get here? One core reason is that the focus of HR has become too strategic.

I understand that there is a need for strategic HR in large organisations to influence the development and growth of employees, bring in new talent, and ensure that profit is not the only issue on the board's agenda. However, sets of values, staff surveys and forums at times make it feel like we as HR professionals follow processes just to tick boxes. We collate feedback from surveys, but do we actually have the time to listen to what really matters to our individual colleagues? Often, the business owner is happy if we have simply conducted the survey. But what do we do with the results from the survey?

Some HR companies offer retainer contracts to help smaller businesses with the issues raised, which gives small business owners the security of having some-one at the end of a call. Unfortunately, this type of service encourages business owners to be reactive rather than proactive.

In addition, poorly performing HR managers who don't like people are a problem in themselves. Why are they working in HR at all, when HR is about en-gaging with employees and understanding what really matters to them? If an HR professional doesn't fully understand this, how can they serve the em-ployees or the wider business?

We've looked at the challenges here – I hope you haven't been put off from continuing your HR career! Now, let's move on to something a little more posi-tive: how to overcome these issues.

In short, we must create a new HR brand that stands for:

- Making employees feel valued

- Adding value to the business

- Growing with the business

- Teamwork and trust

- Being proactive rather than reactive

- Credibility and expertise

- Building capability

- Staying ahead of the game

That sounds far more motivating.

The HR Brand Blueprint

Throughout my career in HR, working with several thousand employees and managers, I have discovered that there are five areas we need to master to be in HR:

- Partnership

- Process

- Productivity

- Performance

- Progress

As an HR professional, it is important to find a balance of all five of these areas, not just master one or two.

The world is forever changing. Industries are adapting to technological innovations more quickly and millennial employees require something new. They want more, expect more, and have more.

I have witnessed HR professionals who are fantastic at reeling off policies and processes and quick to report who isn't abiding by them. However, they forget to take into consideration the impact these policies and processes may have on people. Business growth comes from growing people within our organisations, investing in their development, helping them to become accountable for their performance, and watching them thrive.

How can you become slicker and more efficient at what you do, and deliver more for your customers, businesses or organisations? How can you ensure that you stay on track and review your progress?

First, you have to build a partnership. Without this, you will fail to gain the respect and trust of the directors and managers you are working with. You will also fail to build a great relationship with the team of employees. If you build the right partnership, your working relationships will transform. You will get the buy-in and engagement you need to direct change, both from the directors and from the employees; you will build a great reputation and HR brand; and you will stay on top of your personal development.

Without process, you will be firefighting every day. You will also be seen as a disorganised individual who is not confident. If you get the process right, you will be in control, you will know exactly how to advise your team when it comes to handling difficult situations, and you will build credibility as an expert. You will be the go-to person.

But that's not all. You will also need productivity. Without this, you will be unclear on your outcomes and the measure of your success. By instilling productivity in the people you work with, you will support the business through providing accurate information and achieving tangible results.

How about performance? I must admit, this is a real passion of mine. Without performance, the business will not grow, and your most talented people will leave. If you get performance right, morale will be high, and people will be accountable for their contribution towards the growth of the business.

And finally, you will need to check on progress. Without progress, you will be unclear on the expectations of your business, organisation or clients, which leaves plenty of room for assumptions and miscommunication. Get progress right, and, as if by magic, you will know what to expect of yourself, your team and your business. Everyone will be clear about what is going on, and you will be able to identify what changes need to take place to keep the business growing.

Now that I've introduced you to these five areas, let's use them to create a respected HR brand within your business. A brand that your directors and managers will respect, and that your team members will appreciate.

Remember – HR is about building a partnership with the people you work with, first and foremost. To help you to build your HR brand, I have developed a unique system called the HR Brand Blueprint:

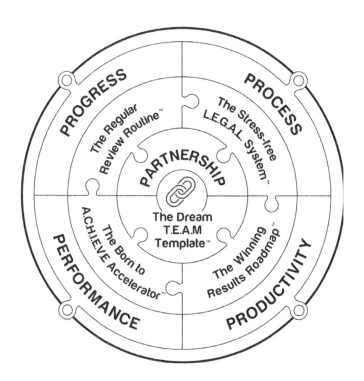

In the next chapter, I will be sharing the four stages of the Dream TEAM template: Tune in, Engagement, Associates and Mindset, along with some great tools which have helped me throughout my HR career. Chapter 3 will cover the hugely important subject of good process management. To help you manage your processes really well, I have developed a simple five-step tool, known as the Stress-free LEGAL System. This tool covers the process steps of Law, Employee cycle, Guides, Audits and Levelling-up.

The Winning Results Formula, which we will meet in Chapter 4, gives you the chance to see how directors and managers would feel about HR if they could appreciate how it can support the growth of their business. This solution will give you the tools to understand your business goals. It will also check that all roles within the business are aligned with achieving those goals and everyone is doing what they should be doing.

The Born to ACHIEVE Accelerator, which we will discuss in detail in Chapter 5, is for you if you want to spend time with motivated people. Do you want to be around high performers? The principles of ACHIEVE – Accountability, Contribution, Hopes, Implement, Educate, Validate and Elevate – will help you develop people within your business and improve talent retention. Your people won't want to leave, because your company will provide everything they need and they will be aligned with their 'why'.

Finally, the Regular Review Routine, which we will discover in Chapter 6, will provide you with the tools necessary to ensure you are making progress. This will give you an understanding of how to get the right feedback at the right time from everyone within the business.

I want to emphasise that at the core of everything we do as HR professionals is how we treat people: how we make our employees feel valued; how we create a great workplace for our teams; and how we engage with them and take the time to understand what matters to them.

Let's build on what we have learned so far.

Summary

HR as a profession is in need of some clarification. Some of the comments about it online and elsewhere portray it as a way of pulling the wool over the eyes of employees for the benefit of management.

My approach is that it's about serving all the people in an organisation, both employees and employers. There's no denying that that's a challenge, but we can serve all the members of an organisation by focusing on the five Ps: Partnership, Process, Productivity, Performance and Progress.

This focus can be implemented by developing and applying policies to build teams, engage management and motivate people.

Let's move on to looking at how to establish and strengthen partnerships.

CHAPTER TWO

Partnership

'Throughout my HR career, I have effectively taken a blended approach. I have never worked alone, and I have always aimed to take people with me wherever I went... literally! I approached my team before they came to me with problems, making the job more enjoyable because I went looking for good news rather than waiting for bad news. I spent my time with line managers in one-to-ones, or talking to staff on the shop floor and in the warehouse.

Our role in HR is to serve the organisation and the people who work for it. Our role is to create a culture of togetherness, breaking down the barriers between employees and management. But before we can be effective in serving the organisation and its people, we need to consider how we relate to the wider team.

> 'You can make more friends in two months by becoming interested in other people than you can in two years by trying to get other people interested in you.'
> — *Dale Carnegie*
>   How to Win Friends and Influence People

Many HR professionals completely miss this crucial aspect, thereby giving HR a poor reputation that none of us want. After all, we know that HR does *not* stand for human remains! However, if you like to arrange your working day in a manner that ensures you work in isolation from the rest of the team, you will not get the buy-in to deliver change.

For me, HR enables the business to connect with its people, and it enables people to connect with the business's customers. How can we make sure we create these partnerships effectively?

Bearing in mind that HR is fundamentally a service role, I created the Dream TEAM template with its four easy to follow steps:

- Tune in

- Engagement

- Associates

- Mindset

Let's get started with Step 1.

Step 1: Tune in

Tuning in is all about discovering more about the business, the business owners, and how you as an HR professional can contribute to their combined growth. If you don't do this well, you will not get the engagement and buy-in to deliver change and you will feel isolated in your role. If you do this well, you will build a great relationship with colleagues at all levels and feel like you are part of the team. When you are working with a highly engaged team, the likelihood is you will enjoy your role.

A self-help tool that I use to facilitate my conversations and achieve buy-in is the Dynamic Discussion model.

Stage 1: Reflect. When you're meeting with your client or manager, know your purpose. What outcomes are you looking for? The ultimate outcome should always be to build a solid relationship of trust and respect. Balance yourself with the intention of building this partnership. Whatever you may have achieved, the meeting is not about how great you are, but about how you are going to serve the person you are speaking to, so leave your ego at the door and walk in with your heart and mind open. Empty your thoughts before you go into the meeting and be ready to receive.

Stage 2: Rapport. Acknowledge the people in the room. Smile, make eye contact, find common ground, match and mirror movements, read the room, and listen.

Stage 3: Receive. This is where you get to ask questions. Here are some questions you may want to ask:

- Why did you create this business?
- What is the company's vision?
- Who else is involved in the business?
- What are the KPIs and company objectives?
- What have been your most important successes?
- What are your challenges?
- What are your expectations of me?

This step is important for building trust and respect. In completing it, you are showing a genuine interest in what the person you are speaking to does, establishing the reason why they created their business, or why their department is vital to the smooth running of the company.

Remember, most people will become animated and alive when they talk about their passion. This is a great opportunity to ask questions about them, too, for example their interests or their family. Really get to know them well.

Stage 4: Reveal. Now you have listened to what matters most to your client or manager and what they need, it's your turn to share more details about yourself. For example:

- Share what you can do to eliminate some of their challenges and how you can make things simpler for your client or manager

- Explain what makes you different from anyone else and the best person to help your client or manager

- Share some personal information. This will establish a deeper trust and perhaps even develop a friendship with your client or manager

- Speak from the heart – be honest and maintain high levels of integrity

Stage 5: Rules. During the meeting, agree on the next steps and some ideal ways of working together, for example:

- How often you will meet

- How you will give feedback

- How you will prioritise challenges

- How you will give and receive feedback

Often, people are quick to reveal information about themselves, and many HR professionals go straight to Stage 4: Reveal. If you do this, though, your client or manager will likely not be properly in tune with you. Think of a time when you met with someone and, without trying to get to know you first, they asked you for information or leads. Or perhaps they handed over their business card immediately. How did that feel?

Now ask yourself how much time you spend getting to know the business and its people when you start working with an organisation.

The Dynamic Discussion model can be used in any conversation that you have, even outside of work, when you want to convey a message. Just remember to make it your priority to establish where your audience is first. Step into their world.

Go the extra mile: get to know the business and the people first. Treat every client, director and manager as your priority, and you will become more than just an email address people use when they want to complain.

This takes us on to Step 2 of the Dream TEAM Template.

Step 2: Engagement

'There is no magic formula for creating great company culture. The key is just to treat your staff how you would like to be treated.'
— *Sir Richard Branson*

Great engagement means that HR will be seen as a service that all employees and managers within your business can benefit from. If you do this stage well, you will create a strong culture and a highly engaged team, and build credibility. On the flip side, bad engagement means that HR will be seen as a joke.

As I have mentioned and will continue to reiterate, HR has a service function. We as HR professionals serve the people and the community within a business. We provide information, offer advice, train, coach, mentor and offer emotional support, and we are often the people other people feel they can talk to without judgement.

The HR role, however, is not one of office agony aunt. Instead, it is more about coaching people to find their own answers. An effective HR professional knows exactly which questions to ask and will coach managers to create the right culture, ensuring they are examples of what the right culture looks like.

To explain further, I want to introduce you to two exciting concepts at this point. They are servant-leadership and emotional intelligence.

While servant-leadership itself is a timeless concept, the actual phrase was coined by Robert K Greenleaf in 'The Servant as Leader', an essay that he first published in 1970.

> 'The servant-leader is a servant first... It begins with the natural feeling that one wants to serve first. Then, conscious choice brings one to aspire to lead.'
> — *Robert K Greenleaf*
>   The Servant as Leader

Richard Branson is a great example of a servant-leader. He uses emotional intelligence to serve his team first, making his team and his colleagues feel important. But even well-recognised servant-leaders like Richard Branson aren't able to communicate positive messages completely on their own. We all need to be ambassadors of positivity, and making people feel valued should be at the core of what we do.

I propose that we blend in. Let's look for good news rather than wait for bad news to come our way. Let's have face-to-face conversations with our teams, line managers and directors.

How much time do you spend in your own me-centred world? If you can, observe how you judge other people according to your own opinion of what's right (something we are all guilty of from time to time). Bereavement issues are a good example of how HR professionals can sometimes lose touch with the reality of people's lives. Most policies state that we should only allow a maximum of five days' leave for bereavement, and then only for immediate family members, so we unthinkingly beat the HR policy drum. Meanwhile, our colleague may have been close to their uncle/granny/cousin and distraught at the loss. Or perhaps the deceased lived abroad and they will need to travel overseas for the funeral.

Now think how that colleague may feel if the company were to support them properly through an extremely difficult time. In our role as HR professionals, it is our duty – and perhaps also our privilege – to be of service, and to do whatever it takes to make life easier for the people we are working with.

The second exciting concept I would like to discuss here is emotional intelligence.

Salovey and Mayer proposed a model that identified four different factors of emotional intelligence: emotional perception, the ability to reason using emotions, the ability to understand emotions, and the ability to manage emotions.[1]

For me, and many others, emotional intelligence is about understanding people and what matters to them. It is understanding that every individual in the workplace is different. Have you ever judged a person for not being up to your own standards, when in reality, their skills, experience and background are completely different from yours? Take some time to observe and recognise the differences among the colleagues you work with. What do you really know about them?

To give you an example, in my first appointment as HR manager, I noticed that there were a number of colleagues in my store who observed Ramadan fasting. They broke their fast at 4pm, but the staff restaurant finished serving lunch at 2pm, and didn't serve evening meals until much later. My solution was to ask the staff restaurant manager to organise hot meals to be ready at 4pm throughout the month of Ramadan.

In another example, I was working with a colleague who was amazing at his job. He was leading his team and delivering his targets, but unfortunately,

---

1   www.theeiinstitute.com/what-is-emotional-intelligence/4-mayer-and-salovey-model-of-emotional-intelligence.html

his limited understanding of English kept him from being promoted. My solution was to spend some time with him, creating role-play videos of possible interview answers that he could give, all based on his experience. He went home and practised – and he passed his next promotional interview.

Of course, there were times when I encountered difficult situations and what may have seemed to be unruly behaviour from employees. However, at no point did I disrespect or humiliate them. We all, I'm sure, know how important it is to give feedback to help people grow and develop. What is of key importance, though, is how such feedback is delivered.

For example, on one particular day, I was walking the shop floor with one of the line managers when we came across a colleague. We'll call him Bob. I asked Bob what he was working on and made a request that he would refill a stack of beer. In response, Bob became rude and aggressive – right there on the shop floor – and then walked off.

I left him to stew for a while, then asked him to meet me for a coffee.

'What's up, Bob? Is there something on your mind?'

Bob told me that he was feeling tense about a personal situation at home, and that he hadn't been feeling well recently. I listened to him and showed concern by offering to support him in any way I could. I then brought up the important issue of his behaviour.

'Bob, when we were on the shop floor, you came across as rude and disrespectful. Do you think I would ever speak to you in that way?'

Bob looked at me, shamefaced.

'No, you wouldn't, and I'm sorry I behaved like that. It won't happen again, Su.'

It follows that if you work in an operational environment, you need to take some time to find out what your colleagues actually do, and what challenges they face. Be present in their area of work; perhaps even work with them from time to time to build a relationship. After our meeting, Bob and I developed more respect for each other, and I was there to support him throughout his illness and consequent passing away.

My simple personal philosophy is that if I don't like doing something, I won't ask somebody else to do it. I made it my mission to learn as much as I could about what I would and wouldn't like to do. Of course, this didn't mean I had to know how to do absolutely everything in the business. Understanding some of the basics is good enough to show our teams that we are with them – that we know something about what they go through every day.

In his book *How to Win Friends and Influence People*, Dale Carnegie states that a basic human need, almost as important as food and shelter, is the desire to feel important. How does it feel when the top people in your organisation remember details about you? Perhaps they remember the names of your children, or the pets you have. Maybe they know your favourite food. It makes you feel good, doesn't it? So as HR professionals, let's do the same for others. Let's make people feel important.

Think of the people in your business about whom you know little and make time to speak to someone different every day. Never underestimate the power of the positive influence you can have on people, and of course, this doesn't simply apply to employees. We can proactively plan to spend time with union reps, line managers, directors and associates whenever possible.

With that in mind, let's check out Step 3 of the Dream TEAM template.

Step 3: Associates

If you do this step well, you have the best chance of building a solid team around you that has your back and will do whatever it takes to support you. If you don't, you will likely feel isolated and unsure of where to turn for help.

There are many networking events held all over the world which aim to bring people from different professions together. Networking strengthens relationships, creates fresh ideas, raises your profile, increases the number of resources you have at hand, and builds the foundations of a solid and supportive team. There are networking groups for just about every area of life, including health and fitness, business and personal development. If you're a parent, for example, you may be able to relate networking to attending toddler groups and listening to ideas and advice from other parents, sharing suggestions about education, healthcare, or even other playgroups.

In short, networking expands your options and choices. Be proactive and find out what else is going on in the world outside your company.

Some associates you may find valuable to include in your network are:

- Training providers

- Solicitors

- Occupational health facilitators

- HR colleagues

- Apprenticeship providers

- Recruitment agencies

- IT support

- Accountants or payroll colleagues

- Pension providers

- Union representatives

- Other managers within the organisation

- Training companies

Make time to meet up with your associates regularly to share best practice and stay current. More often than not, you will pick up new ideas and suggestions about how to do things more simply. I learned a great deal about my own strengths and weaknesses when I met with other HR professionals, constantly raising the bar for my own development.

A wise African proverb says, 'If you want to go fast, go alone. If you want to go far, go together.' I take this to mean that we should never work in isolation. When we work with others, we enhance our own growth and development.

Let's take a look at the final step in the Dream TEAM template.

Step 4: Mindset

Wherever we go, we take ourselves with us. Put simply, there is no getting away from ourselves.

We are all human, so our mood and state of happiness will tend to affect our performance and how we operate, even if it is in a small way. In this step, we will consider our:

- Purpose (why we do what we do)

- Skills and knowledge of HR (our what and how)

- Leadership (the way we behave towards others)

All of these can be captured on a personal development plan. Everyone needs one of these, so we will cover the topic in more detail at the end of this chapter.

To remain at peak performance levels consistently, we need to understand our purpose and why we do what we do. Why do we work so hard? What do we want to achieve in our lives? What do we want to have in our lives? I believe that whatever we do, we need to bring balance into all areas of our lives. How successful would you be at work if you weren't looking after your health properly, or if your personal relationships felt draining?

Let's take a closer look at how balanced our lives are, with some help from a great leadership tool called the Wheel of Life.

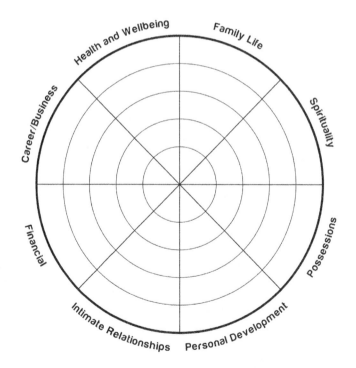

To use the wheel of life effectively, consider how satisfied you feel within each segment, using a scale of 0 = not satisfied at all to 5 = completely satisfied. To help you along the way, let's briefly consider each of these areas by answering some questions.

Health and wellbeing:

- Are you eating healthy food and exercising enough?

- Are you drinking the right amount of fluids?

- Do you have a lot of energy, or are you prone to illness?

- Are you stressed or tired?

Career/business:

- How much do you love what you do?

- Are you ready to move up or change direction in your career?

Family life:

- Do you spend enough time with your children, parents and/or siblings?

- Are there any unresolved conflicts in your relationships with your family or friends?

Spirituality:

(This is not about how religious you are.)

- How satisfied are you with the energy around you?

- Are you generally in a positive or negative state?

Intimate relationships:

- Do you feel loved in your relationship?

- Are you constantly arguing and disagreeing with your partner?

Personal development:

- When was the last time you read a book?

- When was the last time you watched a self-development video?

- When was the last time you attended a workshop or seminar?

Possessions:

- How happy are you with your possessions, such as your house or your car?

- Do you want to own more?

Financial:

- Are you happy with your lifestyle and your standard of living?

- Do you wish you could take more holidays to exotic places?

Once you've finished, take a look at your wheel. Are there any areas that could be more fulfilled? Using the information from your wheel, think about some personal goals you may want to set for yourself and ask yourself why you want to achieve these goals.

Here's an example:

Goal-setting chart

Area	Goal	How	Why I want this
Health	It's September 2018. I am feeling energetic; I weigh 65kgs and I love my body. I am healthy as I eat and drink well and I have a regular exercise routine.	I will join a gym. I will hire a personal trainer. I will create a nutrition plan that supports my lifestyle and diet. I will take action and review my plan with my personal trainer.	To feel more energetic. I want more days of feeling healthy rather than feeling ill. To get more done. To look and feel good about my body. To wear the clothes I like.

Ultimately, we are the only hindrance to living the life we want. Sometimes, we don't achieve our goals because of our limiting beliefs (what we believe to be true about ourselves, such as 'I will always be overweight' or 'I can't learn new skills') and our habits (the patterns we create over time). So how can we break these limiting beliefs?

I have spent most of my life working on eliminating my personal barriers and limiting beliefs, investing a lot of time, energy and money into my development. This is an option that is available to each and every one of us. There are many leadership books available, as well as coaches, workshops and seminars covering almost every subject imaginable. These can all help you break down your own barriers.

Make a commitment and a decision to invest in your development if there is a barrier you want to eliminate. After all, there is only ever going to be one you, so isn't it important to do whatever it takes to be who you want to be and live the life that you want?

HR professionals are great at helping others reach their potential, but we need help too. Having a coach and a mentor is the best investment you will ever make.

HR skills

It is easy for me as an HR professional to preach to others about the skills they need (and believe me, I have met a few HR managers who would agree with this). However, from my experience, most HR professionals don't invest enough time in their own development. But it is not just a matter of investing in our personal growth; we also need to develop our professional selves. HR itself is constantly changing, so we need to keep up and stay ahead of the game.

Many HR professionals wait for their managers to provide them with suggestions for development or training. Others feel they don't have time or that they already have all the skills and knowledge they need. The reality is, there is always more to learn, and in my humble opinion, we as HR professionals need to get better at investing time and money on ourselves. I used to allocate at least one hour every day to my develop-ment, whether that was attending a course, reading a professional article or book, or learning a new skill.

Never stop learning. There are so many opportunities out there, and they will likely open up for you once you get into a solid routine of learning.

If you're looking for a good place to start, here are some examples of the skills you need to develop to be effective in HR.

Skills for HR competence

Technical skills	Leadership skills
• Computer skills – Excel/ Word/PowerPoint	• Influence and change management
• Using social media – LinkedIn, Facebook, Twitter, Instagram	• Delegation, planning and organising
• Employment law	• Teamwork and communication
• Creating people policies and processes	• Solving problems and finding solutions
• HR strategy	• Building relationships
• Organisation structure	• Strategic awareness – knowing your numbers
• KPIs, targets, measures and reporting	• Developing others
• Recruitment and attraction	• Coaching and mentoring
• Training, learning and development	• Training
• Improving performance	• Emotional intelligence
• Reward	• Servant-leadership
• Absence management	• Situational leadership
• Succession planning	
• Managing morale	
• Retention	
• Productivity	

Personal development plan

Everybody – no matter who they are and what level they are working at – needs a continuing personal development plan (PDP). It doesn't need to be complicated, but it should be designed by you, so that you find it both relatable and easy to follow.

A PDP typically comprises the following:

- Improving an area in your life

- Improving your leadership skills

- Improving technical skills

- A clear objective – what is it you want to achieve and why?

- How success will be measured – what does achievement look like to you?

- Action steps – how will you get there?

- Review dates – when will you review your progress?

- Completion date – when will you achieve your outcome?

- What support do you require, and from whom?

- Which courses and qualifications you may want to work towards

Let's take a quick look at all the different methods we
can use to learn or improve our skills:

- Courses

- Qualifications

- Working with a mentor or coach

- Reading books and articles

- Watching videos

- Webinars and online training

- Partnering with others

- Getting involved – having a go

- Practice

- Asking for feedback and reviewing progress

At least one method should suit your lifestyle and
your preferred way of taking in new information, so
if you've been holding back on your development,
there are no more excuses.

Summary

The key message to take from this chapter is that we
as HR professionals need to be proactive. We need to
build great partnerships and take the lead in our own
development.

Manage yourself so that you can continuously improve in your career and your life. Keep in mind that if you don't have a plan of your own, you will end up fulfilling someone else's plan instead. Which would you prefer?

The purpose of the Dream TEAM template is to:

- **Tune in** to the business and build a relationship with the directors and senior managers. Get into their world and share yours by holding dynamic discussions.

- **Engage** and serve the team by using the simple method of talking to them. Be emotionally intelligent and aware by understanding their needs, what motivates them, what they find challenging, what their talents are, and what matters to them.

- Build open relationships with your **associates**.

- Continually work on **mindset** as an HR professional, not just in your professional life, but also in other areas of your life so that you can be the best versions of yourself and maintain great partnerships with your colleagues.

CHAPTER THREE

Process

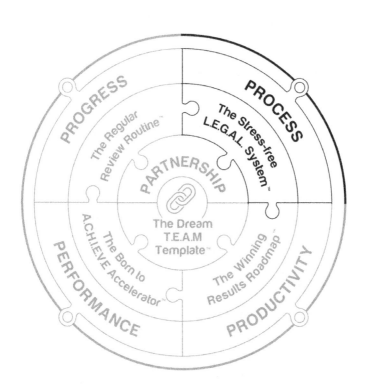

We have spent some valuable time looking at self-development techniques. Now we're going to look at something just as important to an HR career – process.

Though process may not sound particularly glamorous, if you manage it well, you will feel far more confident about the information you provide to your colleagues. Not only will you build credibility, but you will also build a great reputation for caring about your team. On the flipside, if you don't manage process well, you will find yourself constantly firefighting, searching frantically for information and having to work a great deal harder to prove yourself, not to mention establish any credibility.

Let's now look at how to get started on managing process well. To help you achieve this, I have developed a simple five-step tool, the Stress-free LEGAL System. This tool covers the all-important process steps of law, employee cycle, guides, audits and levelling-up.

Step 1: Law

This book is not going to teach you the dull ins and outs of employment law; you can find all the information you need online on supportive websites such as www.acas.org, which belongs to an organisation based in the UK. There are also plenty of free workshops and webinars available, and you will find that government websites include a great deal of legislative information for businesses. Of course, to ensure that your business or organisation is compliant, you regularly need to familiarise yourself with updated legislation.

When I left my corporate role, I quickly realised how much I didn't know. Attending an HR networking meeting, I took part in a quiz about employment law, during which I discovered I didn't know half as much as the HR professionals who worked for smaller organisations. Why was this?

Smaller organisations don't often have legal departments or an all-knowing head of HR to rely on for information. There is nowhere for HR professionals in such organisations to hide; their colleagues expect them to know their stuff, so they make sure they do. I left that meeting feeling quite mediocre, but it was a useful early lesson for me to learn. I wasn't going to let myself feel mediocre in a meeting ever again.

I have since learned that there are just three simple things we need to do to ensure we don't get caught out:

- Know our stuff

- Be proactive

- Communicate

Know your stuff

There are many books on the market with details on HR policy and employment law, but in the face of regularly changing legislation, it is easy for these to become outdated quickly. However, there are many other ways to get up-to-date information about employment law. In addition to the government websites, local law firms often organise free employment law sessions for small businesses, which are great opportunities to network with other HR professionals and business owners.

In the UK, ACAS www.acas.org provides a lot of information and case studies that detail how to manage difficult situations. Additionally, I subscribe to various HR magazines and read up on the latest cases that have been to tribunal. If you can, it is also worth attending a tribunal yourself to get a good feel for what it's like for both parties to go through the procedures of a claim.

Be proactive

Being proactive is all about establishing simple systems, and ensuring information is readily at hand. For example, if you don't know something, be proactive and make it your business to find out, rather than saying something like, 'I didn't do that because I didn't know how to.' Statements of this kind won't win you any credibility.

Being an HR professional isn't about knowing absolutely everything, but about having access to the right information or people with the right information, which is where your network of associates can really support you. Being proactive around your learning and development means you will stay up to date rather than getting caught out for not knowing the basics, so have your policies and simple-to-use templates at hand and easily accessible. Take the initiative to set these up for yourself; don't expect anyone else to do it for you. Make it happen! (It's no accident that being proactive – having a sense of personal responsibility and ownership – ranks as Stephen Covey's top habit in his hugely successful book *7 Habits of Highly Effective People*.)

Communicate

In regard to the Stress-free LEGAL System, communication is about making sure others know and understand how processes and systems work. Contracts of employment and handbooks are great tools for communicating processes to colleagues, but businesses often don't have these basics in place.

In HR, we tend to spend valuable time on creating systems, but we don't communicate or train others in the business on how things work. Alternatively, we will communicate changes, but we don't set the system up. In both of these scenarios, we create confusion and lose credibility.

The answer is simple: train and coach the directors and managers in your business on how to use the systems and procedures, and ensure they understand when to use them. Ensure the information you communicate is simple. Often, we create long-winded briefing packs that nobody reads. Stick to the important parts: namely, what do people need to know, and how does it affect them? Remember that most of the time, people will only want to know about something that directly affects them.

The best method of communication is face to face. In some organisations, HR only communicates with the relevant managers and directors, who are then responsible for sharing the information with their colleagues. By being part of some colleague briefings myself, I was able to ensure they were hearing the right message and that colleagues could ask me questions if they didn't understand anything.

Some people like details, so it's a good idea to provide handouts or leaflets with more information for them to take away. HR is the source of a great deal of company information, so keep an open-door policy for colleagues to ask questions. In fact, if you've been paying attention so far, you'll already have thought about making an effort to seek out colleagues and ask them if they have any questions!

In the HR profession, it's easy to get caught up and overwhelmed with things to do. Our focus takes us straight to legislation and policies, often because we feel vulnerable and unsafe in our own thoughts and opinions. We then end up completing 'easy' tasks just to tick a box.

To keep your professional life stress-free, it's important to prioritise. There are various tools that you may find useful, such as the Eisenhower Decision Matrix – urgent versus important.

I always wanted to work in HR so that I could help grow and inspire people. However, in the early days of my career, I spent more time doing things that had nothing to do with people, such as tracking the company's adherence to policies, general admin, chasing information, responding to emails, and various other tasks that took me away from doing the things I love about HR, such as development meetings with colleagues, one-to-one sessions with line managers, running workshops, coaching and getting to know new colleagues.

With this in mind, review your job description and to-do list. How many tasks involve working with others and are aimed at growing the business compared to firefighting non-growth activities? To find out more about how you can achieve that, let's take a look at Step 2 of the Stress-free LEGAL System.

Step 2: Employee cycle

If you manage the employee cycle well, you will be able to retain talent by understanding the needs of your people and supporting them throughout their careers. If you manage the employee cycle badly, you will lose good talent to your competitors, which will cost your company money.

This step takes up a large section of the book as we spend time looking more closely at the fundamentals of the HR profession. In this section, I am honoured and privileged to include valuable input from specialist guest authors who have taken the time to contribute. I hope they inspire you as much as they have inspired me.

I have worked with many businesses, from start-ups to large corporations, and I have witnessed how often employees are treated like numbers. Time is precious and work is demanding, which means HR departments often opt for an easy one-size-fits-all approach to caring for colleagues.

As an HR professional, one of your key considerations lies in recognising the differences in the skill, experience and background of each colleague, and ensuring that these differences are valued in your business. So how can you go out of your way to ensure each one of your colleagues knows they are important?

In these enlightened times, diversity, inclusion and equality should be a way of life in any business, weaved seamlessly into everything we do within an organisation. Encourage and role-model respect and always take harassment seriously, whether it's based on sex, race, age, sexual orientation, ethnicity and/or disability. View differences as strengths within the business, and value each and every colleague for what they contribute towards its growth.

No matter how skilled they are, all colleagues require training from day one. Make sure your policies are clear about what an employee should do if they encounter discrimination, bullying and harassment, and business leaders need to role-model appropriate behaviour.

While I am positive about encouraging a relaxed and friendly atmosphere at work, be aware that there is an extremely fine line. Particularly in small businesses with small teams, it's easy to fall into the trap of creating a relaxed atmosphere of fun and banter, but no one should ever be made to feel uncomfortable. A workplace needs to be seen as exactly that, so above all else, make sure you cultivate a professional culture.

With just a little effort, at every stage of the employee cycle, you can show your individual colleagues the respect and care they deserve. As a result, employees will thrive in your business, you will build immense loyalty, and your business will grow.

The three stages of the employee cycle are starting, staying and saying goodbye.

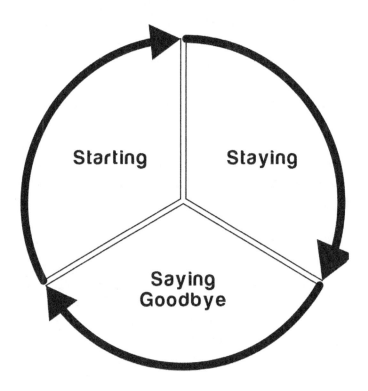

Let's examine the first stage of the employee cycle, and find out exactly what we can do to treat our colleagues like VIPs.

Starting

Many businesses get into a position where they need to employ someone urgently, but this urgency can often be a trigger for mistakes and bad decisions. At best, they take on an employee who turns out to be a potential future leader in the business; at worst, they take on someone who doesn't fit the culture of the business. That person may then try to do whatever it takes to change the culture to fit them instead.

Forecasting. To avoid making too many mistakes, you need to plan for manpower well before you need it. By having a forecasting process in place, you will be able to plan ahead and start the candidate attraction process as soon as possible.

The forecasting process is as simple as reviewing the organisation's structure and asking, 'As a business, where are we going to be in six months? What changes are most likely to impact us? What resources will we need?' Once you know how many resources you are likely to require, the next step is to determine what type of contract you want to have with the people who will be part of your core team.

Types of contracts. There are many different types of contracts to consider when you're recruiting new employees. Each one comes with a different set of rules for the business and entitlements for the employee, so you need to decide what is right for your business and your people.

Some examples are:

- Self-employed

- Zero-hour

- Standard contract of employment

You will need to consider whether positions will be flexible, temporary (for a fixed period of time), or permanent. Finally, consider if the contract will be full time (forty+ hours) or part time.

Use the business and job requirements to help you make your selection. The important aspect is to find the right balance between what the business needs and what is ethical for the individual. Be open and honest from day one about the type of contract you are offering, and ensure you provide the employee with a written contract within four weeks of their start date.

Job description/person specification. You need to describe the expectations of the job clearly in the job description and person specification. This gives your candidate clarity on what the role involves, and then they will be in a better position to match themselves to the job.

Attraction. There are many methods of attracting the right candidates, such as advertising in job centres, recruitment agencies, job boards, internet job searches or apprenticeships. Apprenticeships are gaining popularity again in the UK, and are particularly useful for growing talent and building loyalty right from the beginning of a young person's career.

HR professionals benefit greatly from building strong relationships with recruitment providers and/or sourcing agencies. Find a key contact within each of these businesses and ensure you stay in touch regularly throughout the year.

Whichever method you use to attract employees, always ensure your expectations are clear and transparent. Adverts must provide as much information as possible and be written in a way that showcases your company's culture.

Sometimes, business owners believe that employees should feel privileged to have a job with them. However, as an HR professional, always remember that attracting the right employees is a two-way process. Take a few moments to think about the reasons why a candidate may be attracted to your company over your competitors'.

Things to consider:

- Training/mentoring

- Opportunities and variety

- Progression/career advancement

- Social factors

- Pay

- Benefits

- Bonus schemes

- Leave entitlements

Recruitment. During the recruitment process, communication is fundamental. Candidates need to know what they are expected to do, what will happen at every stage of the recruitment process, and the eventual outcome. I really want to emphasise here that candidate care must be at the top of your priority list when it comes to recruitment. Whether you offer a candidate a job or not, ensure they leave the process feeling like they have been treated with care and respect. Consider the possibility that even if a candidate is not suitable for the advertised role, they may be suited to an alternative position.

Selection. When you're selecting your candidates, ensure each one has received a copy of the job description beforehand so that they can match themselves to the job and prepare for the interview. Usually, the selection process consists of an application form or a CV, and an interview and/or an assessment. There is no definitive right way to do it, but whichever method you use, ensure you always provide feedback to the candidates. Your company's reputation depends on the feedback it receives, so don't leave any candidate feeling as though they have had a bad experience with your business.

You can give feedback over the phone, via email or in a letter. However the candidates may have performed during your selection process, make sure you let every one of them know their results.

Interviews. Interviews need to be fair and consistent. Sitting down over coffee and having a rushed, informal chat won't highlight anybody's key strengths, but helping your candidate to feel relaxed from the start of their interview will go a long way towards ensuring the interview runs smoothly. Begin by asking questions about the candidate, their family, their personal goals – and don't forget to share some information about yourself, too. Endeavour to understand their world and let them into yours.

This opening could be followed by a selection of behavioural or competency-based interview questions. For the purpose of providing accurate feedback later on and to ensure consistency, take notes. Even better, take some time to write up a brief summary after each interview.

Assessments. While online assessments are a fantastic tool for finding further information about a candidate in terms of their strengths and development needs, I feel that they are too impersonal. Additionally, I'm yet to be fully convinced that they consistently provide accurate information.

I remember once being asked to follow a test to determine my own strengths. I left with the impression that I had done quite well, but I later discovered that my score was low in key business areas. After she'd had a more detailed conversation with me, my interviewer – let's call her Liz – decided to go with her gut feeling and give me the opportunity anyway, and I did not let her down. In fact, I felt extremely loyal towards her, and I wanted to prove to myself that the areas the assessment had highlighted as development needs were going to become my top strengths. Needless to say, Liz would have missed out on a great opportunity to work with me if she had made a decision based only on the results of that online assessment.

Feedback. Explain your feedback to unsuccessful candidates. Whichever method you choose to deliver your feedback (email is acceptable, and makes the process quick and easy), it is absolutely imperative that you at least let candidates know they have not been successful. If a candidate asks for additional feedback, refer to your notes and provide this in a professional and objective manner. I will sometimes ask how the candidate felt about the process to help them identify any areas in which they could have done better.

Congratulate the successful candidates and send them an offer letter inviting them to their induction day.

Legal checks and documents. Before we move on, I want to make a quick point about key legal checks. Depending on which country your business operates in, you may be required to carry out legal checks before you employ someone. This may begin with an immigration check, meaning candidates must be asked to bring any immigration documents to their interview so that you can make a copy. Do not formalise job offers until you've seen, copied and acknowledged these documents with a signature.

Your government website will provide you with a list of valid documents to help you identify and conduct any relevant checks. Note that if your business works with vulnerable people, you may be required to submit further validated information. Whatever the outcome is of any checks you make, you must ensure that you maintain the good reputation of your business by treating everybody concerned with respect and dignity.

Induction. At this point, you will have completed the hard recruitment work and found a colleague who is the right fit for your business – well done! Now it's time to remember that what you do in the first few weeks will determine your colleague's perception of your business, and how long they may decide to work there.

> 'Research suggests that new employees decide whether or not they feel welcome in the workplace within the first 30 days. To retain and engage them, the company needs to leverage the enthusiasm, energy, and excitement they bring to the staff.'
> — *Sharon Armstrong and Barbara Mitchell*
>   The Essential HR Handbook

Every company will have its own induction pro-gramme, which is usually facilitated or at least attended by the HR manager. For me, this is the re-warding part of the role: I get to meet the company's new recruits. Remember that you as an HR profes-sional are the face of the organisation, so new recruits need to know whom to approach if they have any issues. This will immediately put them at ease and make them feel like they can contribute to the com-pany in a positive way.

An induction is usually a one- or two-day event that covers the company's history, vision, policies and procedures, and safety in the workplace, followed by a detailed orientation of the departments relevant to the new recruit and an introduction to the team. For me, though, the best induction programmes are run over a period of twelve weeks. These incorporate detailed training, validations, performance reviews, and opportunities for new recruits to share ideas in staff sessions and forums. Ideally, the induction includes at least one informal social event.

A note about emotional intelligence. You may have already established that emotional intelligence is key in the starting stage of the employee cycle. As leaders, we need to use our own emotional intelligence to understand whether or not a candidate is the right fit for the business. It almost goes without saying that we look to recruit based on attitude rather than skills and experience. Skills and experience can be learned over time; the ideal candidate will have an attitude that complements your business and the role they are applying for. Having said that, it's important to be open minded here: a good mix of backgrounds, personalities and traits brings substance to any team.

Emotional intelligence is also necessary to understand how a new colleague is settling in and identify anything they may need. In short, if people feel connected and valued from day one, and you have supported them throughout the initial weeks of their induction, they are more likely to stay with your company.

Staying

Instilling a genuine sense of belonging will help to build loyalty in a colleague, so if you have carried out a meaningful induction programme over the first twelve weeks of their employee cycle, they should feel settled and part of the team. Conversely, keeping great colleagues will be a challenge if you use a one-size-fits-all approach.

Let's take a more in-depth look at what we can do to retain great talent in our business.

Leadership. We touched on the concept of servant-leadership in the previous chapter. For me, servant-leadership is about putting our colleagues first, treating them as individuals, and applying emotional intelligence regarding their needs and our impact upon them.

Leaders often encounter problems when they let their egos get in the way. HR can help counter the negative effects of ego-dominance by ensuring leaders are properly trained to use emotional intelligence and servant-leadership techniques.

Communication. Much of this book is about communication, which underlines its importance in business – you can never communicate too much. Certainly, if you keep talented people in the know about what's going on in your company, you will help to keep them engaged and motivated.

The best communication takes place in person, which is something I encourage managers to facilitate as much as possible. As a quick and easy example, the companies I have worked with hold ten-minute team talks, during which we gather colleagues and managers together for a quick huddle to share relevant information. We also communicate regularly through newsletters, notice boards and longer staff sessions.

Always consider meeting colleagues in person to share information as opposed to sending faceless emails. The email option may seem easier, but the personal approach can be so much more rewarding for everybody involved.

Benefits and reward schemes. Many companies spend a lot of money on developing employee benefits and reward schemes, which are seen as vitally important factors in retaining good people. However, the most important and potentially successful aspect of benefits and reward schemes is not money, but consideration of employee needs.

Before you implement a new scheme, consider asking your employees what benefits and rewards matter most to them. Clearly, there is no point introducing a scheme that is not relevant to your employees' lives and concerns. Not only will this make them feel as though you have not bothered to listen to them, the scheme will also not motivate or engage them. It may even have the opposite effect.

I once worked with a company that introduced a benefits scheme that consisted of days out and money-off vouchers. Most of the employees worked full time, for six or seven days a week, plus overtime. Many had been born in countries outside the UK, and the majority worked long and hard to send money back home. When holiday time came, they would visit family in their home countries. These employees did not value a benefits scheme that prioritised days out and discount vouchers. Indeed, their feedback stated that they would not make use of the new benefits system.

When we consider this issue with an objective and honest approach, it is clear that benefit schemes must support the lifestyle and interests of the employees involved in order for them to represent true benefits.

Pay and reward schemes. In my opinion, if you offer a set pay increase every year, you encourage mediocrity and complacency. I love the idea of everybody being accountable for their own performance, so a reward scheme should be exactly that – employees will be rewarded for the contribution they make. Though this is challenging to implement at first, it is a fair and balanced system that ensures the best reward for individual employees, all with individual needs, hopes and ambitions. When we put everyone in one large box, disengagement often follows – and the consequences of this is much more challenging to manage than a contribution-based reward scheme.

Performance management. As we will cover this topic in detail later in the book, the one important point I'd like to make now is that *nobody* comes to work to do a bad job. However, I have found that employees often under-perform because we as leaders are not managing or leading them as well as we could. In every performance management situation I have been involved in, the manager has failed the employee in some way, whether through not setting clear expectations, withholding training, or simply not listening.

It's easy to underestimate the positive effects of praise when a colleague has done something well, so make sure you offer praise wherever you can and encourage other leaders to do the same.

Appraisals. In large companies, there has been talk about abolishing appraisal meetings. It's easy to understand this viewpoint when we consider that such meetings are held just once or twice a year at best. From those I've witnessed, there is little or no follow-up, and a lack of continuity. In addition, the process is often subjective; managers may sometimes feel inclined to base feedback or grading on the perceived likeability of a colleague, instead of taking an objective view of their performance.

Working in the SME world, I've found that unless the business owner is a natural leader of people, appraisal processes just do not happen. Sometimes with the business owner expecting their employees' self-motivation and drive to sit at the same high level as their own.

My view is that appraisals are an absolute must. Not everybody is self-motivated or driven, so when it's executed well, the appraisal meeting represents a golden opportunity to help colleagues train and learn to take accountability for their performance, as well as recognise and showcase their contribution to the business. It is also a wonderful opportunity for any leader to give personal recognition, acknowledgement and praise to their team members.

Companies therefore need to commit to their appraisal process, and not limit discussions to once a year. The progress and outcomes of the reviews must be discussed in regular one-to-one meetings throughout the year, ensuring development, learning and contribution is kept at the top of the agenda. The role of HR in this instance is to create a meaningful appraisal review document that facilitates an open conversation and to train managers on the importance of conducting fair and effective review meetings.

Absence and wellbeing. These days, more and more businesses take a proactive approach to employee wellbeing. Yours could very well be one of them.

According to a survey carried out by Virgin Pulse in 2016, more employers are offering packages that seek to improve their workers' overall wellbeing, including physical, mental, social and emotional aspects. This approach can work extremely well when it is properly role-modelled and facilitated by the leadership team. At best, employers are educating colleagues on health and wellbeing, encouraging prevention as the cure. At worst, though, employers are disapproving of or even disciplining colleagues for taking time off work due to illness.

We in HR are not doctors, so it is not our job to question colleagues around the perceived authenticity of their sick leave. However, in cases of persistent absence, we do need to make sure we have a fair and consistent process in place. This usually includes a notification of absence process, a return to work process, and an investigation and eventually disciplinary process for persistently unacceptable levels of absence.

I believe that prevention is indeed the cure, so wherever possible, our first response to 'May I book a day off?' should involve finding a way to make it possible. With regard to sickness levels, helping colleagues to take full accountability for their attendance is key.

The mental health charity, MIND, offers a guide for colleagues entitled 'Wellness Action Plans'. This provides vital and practical information about how to stay well at work, together with a template that helps promote personal awareness of mental health. I used this fantastic document as a model for my own practical health guide, which I produced to help colleagues learn how to stay well in four areas – physical, mental, social and emotional health. This gave them accountability for their own attendance and formed part of their PDP.

Physical wellness. Don't forget to ask your colleagues about the wellbeing support they would most like. To help you get started, here are some ideas:

- Offer gym memberships, working with local trainers and gyms to get discounted corporate rates

- Provide easy-to-use and simple gym equipment in communal areas

- Organise walking clubs at lunchtime

- Ask colleagues to sign up for a company football/netball team

- Organise a colleague sports day

- Provide colleagues with information about the benefits of physical activity

Mental wellness. Mental health is not always taken seriously in work environments. Certain mental health issues can even result in colleagues feeling judged for being lazy or not fit for the job they are doing. However, through being proactive, we can support our colleagues to boost their mental health. Here's how:

- Regular reviews will keep the conversation open, giving colleagues an opportunity to share anything on their mind

- Realistic goal-setting will help colleagues find a sense of purpose in their role

- Recognition – do lots of celebrating with colleagues and create a positive environment

- Collaboration – organise team events and meetings where colleagues can feel part of a supportive group

- Training and education – create a space where colleagues can learn and stimulate their minds in areas outside of their job description

Social wellness. Not everyone is confident in a social environment, and some may shy away from interaction. Here are some ways to help them get more involved:

- Encourage charity work – volunteering time to support others with their skills

- Organise social events

- Organise special event days at work, such as competitions, fancy dress or quizzes

- Offer coaching or training in self-confidence

- Help colleagues to create a PDP to work on their personal skills

- Provide self-development books and regular information

Emotional wellness. Emotional people can be unfairly seen as unprofessional and potentially volatile. We need to recognise that over-emotional responses can often be triggered by events at work that do not support emotional wellbeing.

Here are a few questions that will help you encourage emotional wellness in your company:

- Does the leadership team acknowledge colleagues with a warm and welcoming greeting at the start of their shift?

- Are colleagues thanked for their time and effort at the end of their shift?

- Is there any opportunity to offer flexible working?

- Are colleagues completely engaged in the company's mission? Do they have a sense of purpose and contribution?

- Are colleagues allowed free use of technology, or are they blocked from using their phones?

- Do colleagues have an area where they can spend casual time with their workmates?

People tend to remember the times when they have been shown compassion at work. When my daughter was very young, she became ill and I had to take some time off work to take care of her. I asked my manager if I could take some annual leave to look after my daughter.

Her empathetic response was, 'How is caring for somebody else a holiday for you?' She refused me the annual leave, instead telling me to take as much time as I needed and paying me my usual wage for the whole time I spent caring for my daughter. You may imagine how grateful, committed and loyal I felt in response to her trust and compassion, and I hope this story inspires you to encourage the same environment in your company.

Training colleagues and managers. In your service to other functions across the business, you will need to work alongside managers to identify gaps in training. Colleague training is generally easier to conduct than management training because new colleagues are often buddied up with more experienced colleagues. Experience doesn't necessarily equal expertise, though. Don't take it for granted that all colleagues have received the right training and understand your company's goals and expectations simply because they have worked in the business for a long time. I set up tracking systems on spreadsheets to monitor training and progress with managers. I don't know about you, but I love a good tracker!

HR also has a duty to ensure that managers are trained on how to manage people and processes effectively. This is another aspect that can be taken for granted, with companies often not investing appropriate amounts of time and money on the development of managers.

Management training can be executed in house if you are a qualified trainer, or it can be outsourced. Throughout my career, I have agreed detailed training plans with individual managers during scheduled meetings, and I have also encouraged managers and staff to take accountability for their own learning.

I would now like to introduce you to one of my valued contributors who is a dear friend and associate of mine. Ross Trigwell, founder of The Learning and Development Company, is a man of many talents. He is passionate about the work he does with business managers, and it shows. His workshops are inspirational, providing managers with clarity on becoming a leader of the future.

Ross has created an accredited world-class brand in which he exceeds the expectations of his delegates. Not only that, he follows up all of his courses with an effective post-course support system that I have never seen provided by any other company.

Ross is the humblest man I have ever worked with. He is authentic, full of integrity, and he really cares about the people he works with.

PLANNING TO DEVELOP OUR FUTURE LEADERS

When it comes to training our leaders and their teams, I highly recommend a well-engineered plan.

Spreadsheets at the ready! Work with senior managers and stakeholders to help you form a skills gap analysis or skills matrix covering leadership and technical areas. A non-negotiable is that leaders/managers actually want to be leaders/managers. If they do not, you'll be up against it (so check that you're recruiting the right people). The same goes for their team members: willingness is paramount. If your future leaders are trainable, open and coachable, they'll be on a far better footing for providing day-to-day development for their teams.

Training should provide managers with the tools and the confidence they need to develop individuals and teams back in the business.

Consider how you will measure your return on investment. Communication with seniors and stakeholders will help you align improvements (or lack thereof) to an individual's performance over a period of months. Your boss or CEO is likely to want to know how training and development initiatives are impacting on the bottom line. My advice is to start with the end in mind. Don't just send people on training courses; have a plan and be an expert in communicating the tangible benefits. Ensure you have the conversation about measuring return on investment with any prospective training provider.

Here is a checklist you may find useful:

- Construct a skills matrix that incorporates leadership and technical training
- Develop or invest in a well-put-together modular leadership and management development programme
- Make sure your programme includes interim learning opportunities and is not too heavy on theory – keep it practical

- Align training initiatives with business goals and objectives
- Start with the end in mind – become an expert at measuring return on investment
- Encourage managers to use internal resources, such as buddying experienced colleagues with new learners
- Where possible, deploy a top-down approach to leadership development
- Check colleagues' willingness to learn
- Recruit the right people

Ross Trigwell, founder of
The Learning and Development Company

Annual leave. You may recognise a general pattern for annual leave: usually slow at the start of the year, high during school holidays, slow again, and then very high towards the end of the holiday year as colleagues want to take their leave entitlement before it's too late. The problem with this way of managing holidays is that colleagues are often disappointed if they can't take the dates they require and/or the business has too many colleagues off at the same time. This puts pressure on other colleagues, ultimately affecting the level of service the business provides to customers.

If this method works for your business, go with the flow. However, I like to keep things simple by being proactive. You can plan annual leave in advance of the holiday year, allowing some flexibility for emergencies. Of course, the culture within an organisation must encourage such flexibility. On a first come, first served basis, encourage colleagues to provide their annual leave dates as early as possible, so they can secure the right time. You can then track the requests using an HR information software system, or by using a simple holiday chart tracker if your business is small.

Depending on your location, there may be legal requirements that govern the minimum amount of annual leave an employee is entitled to.

In HR, our role is to update managers with the information they need to manage all these requirements effectively.

Recognition. It's time to introduce another contributor and dear friend of mine. Kalpesh Patel is truly the enlightened entrepreneur. He really understands people with a deep level of compassion I have rarely observed in others. His whole reason for being lies in transforming the way people think so they can plan a positive future. He has certainly transformed my thinking, and with his mentoring and coaching, I have grown not only as an entrepreneur, but also as an individual who focuses on others.

Wherever Kalpesh goes, he meets people he has worked with and transformed in some way. He meets people who not only respect him for what he does but love him for who he is. I very much hope you get to meet him one day, too.

THE MAGIC OF RECOGNITION

Firstly, thank you for reading my favourite section of this book – I will confess I'm slightly biased! I hope you will feel inspired by the end of it.

When Su first shared her vision for her new company, I knew from her conviction and tone that she was about to do something amazing in a way that only she could. You can imagine my delight when Su asked if I would write a piece on a subject dear to my own heart. It has inspired me to stretch way beyond my own limits throughout my life.

That subject is recognition. Children cry for it; teens rebel for it; gangs kill for it; soldiers die for it; workers lie for it; and adults compromise their values for it. Our insatiable craving for recognition follows us into our personal lives, friendships, relationships and – believe it or not – the workplace.

The need for recognition starts from a young age. If we do not receive much of it, the negative effects can be devastating and long lasting. Children are often told to get out of the way, to stop making noise, or go and play upstairs, and this creates a feeling of abandonment in them which can and usually does lead to negative self-belief. Our world gets smaller as we get bigger, and soon enough, a dysfunctional and insecure adult emerges.

Limiting beliefs stem from the way we interpret events that take place in our lives. Humans are generally good at destroying their own self-image. This then becomes a default thought process that we don't even realise is happening.

I often say that the damage was done long before someone else triggered it. Our 'stinking thinking' and negative self-talk hides itself comfortably in our subconscious mind, eating away all that is great. Many of us suffer from a negative attitude, self-image and self-talk; we put ourselves down and then look for references to confirm our own insecurities in the form of other people's opinions of us.

At work, the magic of recognition dilutes as it filters through an organisation's ranks, from top management to the lowest paid employee – if it even gets that far. But everybody wants to be seen, heard, and acknowledged for their existence in their own eco-system. Therefore, a well-designed, well-oiled, well-structured and, most importantly, well-implemented and maintained recognition programme is invaluable to the long-term success of any company. It reduces staff attrition and days off, and achieves more fun and efficiency. This is such an obvious strategy that benefits everybody, and yet it is rarely taken seriously or executed properly by HR.

I have been blessed to have worked in dozens of countries, teaching many leaders and influencers the importance of recognition in their organisations. Some people believe in fate, others believe in karma, some believe in themselves, but unfortunately, most believe in what others think of them. This is even more prevalent with the explosion of social media, on which people are so desperate to get likes and comments that their self-worth and esteem depend on it.

I remember when I was around five years old, my parents would tell me and others that I was a gifted child. One day, they said that I would be a successful businessman, travel the world and make a huge difference. Well, guess what? I believed them, and the rest, as they say, is his-story.

When we really think about it, adults are no different to children. If your lover, sibling, business partner, work colleague or boss talks you down, disempowers you and finds fault, you can launch into a downward spiral of behaviour that leads to a lack of interest, focus, participation and, in many cases, stress, anger, frustration, anxiety and even depression. Equally, when someone acknowledges your behaviour, quality of work, productivity, performance, improvements, abilities, skills or knowledge, you instantly feel great. Something inside lights up, triggering positive behaviour. Secure in yourself, you may go on to improve on what you have already achieved. Knowing how obvious this basic human behaviour is, I am astonished to observe how most corporations and management-level workers fail to capitalise on it.

There is a huge lack of genuine understanding. Companies spend millions on getting it totally wrong.

Have you ever noticed how a couple can thrive in the early stages of a relationship, and then start to dive once the honeymoon period passes? It's because at the start, they focus on each other's greatness, even recognising the smallest things as great. They smother each other with compliments about their dress sense, their laugh, their voice, their eyes, their smile, their everything. Over time, though, they take for granted the very things they once recognised as beautiful, and eventually they begin to get on each other's nerves. Their focus shifts away from gratitude and recognition, leading to a plateau in the relationship, peppered with put-downs and fault-finding.

By contrast, recognition rewards both the recipient and the provider infinitely in ways that cannot be quantified, going way beyond the bottom line. A compound effect takes place between people who acknowledge each other, and this allows all to grow and flourish much faster than they would otherwise.

Kalpesh Patel, Top 100 speaker, transformational thinking trainer and enlightened entrepreneur

---

I hope Kalpesh's inspirational contribution sparks thoughts and ideas in you about how to give recognition freely and generously. For me, recognition is the heartbeat of long-term loyalty and success in any relationship, especially in business. Leaders often forget to put making their team feel valued at the top of their agenda. They must build elevating and lifting other people, recognising them for the value they add and the contribution they make, into every communication.

I love working in HR because one of my key priorities is to help business owners, leaders and management teams implement regular recognition, thereby demonstrating its power. Over the years, I have witnessed many of my clients excel at recognising their colleagues. Please don't underestimate the impact of recognition on your business. It can have a huge positive effect on performance, innovation, service and many other vital areas.

As ever, Dale Carnegie sums it up perfectly in *How to Win Friends and Influence People,* identifying one longing that is as deep as the desire for food and sleep: the desire to be important, which is often not gratified.

> 'Leaders don't look for recognition from others, leaders look for others to recognise.'
> — *Simon Sinek*

In my former employment, we in HR recognised colleagues who provided outstanding customer service. We bought them a personalised gift and acknowledged them in our team talks. One of my clients celebrates each colleague individually for one thing they have contributed during the year with a handwritten thank you card and gift. Being specific and personal makes this kind of acknowledgement far more meaningful.

Coaching managers and directors in providing day-to-day recognition doesn't have to be complicated. While you can never overdo recognition, my advice is to keep it simple.

Here are a few tips to get you started right away, at zero cost:

- Verbal praise
- Handwritten notes
- Emails to say thank you and well done
- A public notice in the staff area
- Certificates of achievement
- A special lunch with the director
- Celebrate birthdays
- Celebrate personal achievements
- Celebrate service awards
- Employee of the month ceremonies

I hope I've made a resonating point about the importance of recognising people. If nothing else, you may be able to tell that recognition is one of my main areas of passion.

When a team works in perfect synergy, it will operate at a level that multiplies in value over time. When this happens, the rewards to the company go far beyond any cost.

Being family friendly. Having a family is an exciting time, yet it can be worrying for employees in terms of how a baby will affect other areas of life, such as finances, work and those all-important energy levels.

During my career in HR, as soon as a colleague announced that they were having a baby, I made sure I congratulated them. I also arranged a meeting to reassure them, encouraging them to ask any questions. This was a great time to carry out a simple risk assessment, check dates for leave and confirm pay over the leave period.

By arranging a meeting immediately, you can reassure your colleagues so that they will know what to do and what to expect. If you make a positive fuss about a new baby arriving, not just for expectant mums, but for dads and grandparents, too, you will make them feel valued and supported.

As much as starting a family represents a seismic change in most people's lives, so do separation and divorce. Although these are often seen as personal, private issues that should not affect the workplace, if you offer support during stressful family-related events, you will relieve emotional pressure from a colleague, allowing them to feel safe and secure.

I would now like to introduce my next contributor, Suzy Miller. Another dear friend of mine and an inspiration in herself, Suzy is a mover and a shaker in her field. I admire her mostly for her tenacity – if there is something she doesn't know how to do, she will give it a go and eventually become its master.

Suzy is a divorce strategist who collaborates with the Ministry of Justice in promoting mediation and other forms of dispute resolution as preferable routes through divorce. She has written extensively about healthy co-parenting and better ways to divorce for national magazines, the *Huffington Post* and the *Daily Mail*.

Suzy has overcome many personal challenges and has an amazingly positive outlook on life and the people around her. She is passionate about building and maintaining relationships and is a definite force to be reckoned with.

DIVORCE IS HURTING BRITISH WORKPLACES

'Companies should intervene and help
employees going through marital break-ups to
prevent them "crashing out" of work and ending
up on benefits, Iain Duncan Smith has said.'
  — *Daily Telegraph*
    26 November 2014

Has anything changed since 2014?

No, it hasn't. Despite the fact that family break-
ups and divorce bring with them significant health
consequences, both physically and emotionally
– making it vital that colleagues and managers
have a basic understanding of how to deliver
emotional first aid – access to this training is
not generally provided. Divorce-related stress
is made far worse by the situation possibly
becoming adversarial, and the financial strains
and sometimes separation from the children
can lead to absenteeism and self-destructive
behaviour in employees who are affected.

'One in ten have had to leave jobs after a
split, or have a colleague who has ...'[2]

A happy workforce provides more return on
investment to the company, but how do you

2   'Divorce Hurting British Workplaces', *Daily Telegraph*, 26 November
     2014.

proactively reduce the influence of stress
caused by factors outside of the workplace?

In the UK, between 15,000 and 20,000 couples go
to court to resolve child access disputes each year.
In a survey by Mishcon de Reya, one in five parents
admitted that their primary objective was to make
the experience 'as unpleasant as possible' for their
former spouse, even when they knew that this
would make the situation worse for their children.

I believe that making divorce first aid available to
employees to share with their families, in the form
of coaching and counselling, will have a positive
preventative effect. Some who access the free
introductory sessions may end up not getting
divorced at all, while others will find a more amicable
way to go through the process, or at least not get
sucked in to their ex-partner's aggressive approach.
There will also be beneficial effects on mental health.

'One in five men is at risk of depression at
the onset of divorce and separation...'[3]

Men are at more than twice the risk of suicide after
divorce than women, and many children self-harm
because of their parents' angry breakup. Anecdotally,
I have often heard of high-level employees taking
time off work for 'stress' which has been caused
by the psychological impacts of a nasty divorce.

---

3   'Divorce Hurting British Workplaces', *Daily Telegraph*, 26 November
     2014.

Stress is the number one reason for absenteeism
at work, and clearly, simply providing access
to a counselling telephone line is not going
to cut it. Even back in 2008, courts were
taking a stand against such complacency.

'The court made it clear that if an employee
tells her employer she is suffering from stress
and cannot cope, it is not an adequate response
merely to tell her to seek counselling.'
— *Personnel Today*
   2008

Through divorce first aid, companies can add
something unique and valuable to their employee
wellbeing provision – something that I believe
will have a significant impact on reducing the
continuing rise in stress-related absence and
mental illness suffered by many companies in
the UK. Divorce impacts the workplace heavily
because it increases financial pressures, emotional
turmoil, and absence rates in employees – and
this impacts the company's bottom line directly.

While new ways of signposting and supporting
employees through a range of everyday life crises
do exist, too many companies are still trying to
pretend that their existing employee assistance
programmes (EAPs) are sufficient for supporting
employees who are tackling divorce and family
separation. In addition, prevention strategies such
as signposting employees towards free online
resources mostly do not exist. One could be

forgiven for believing that 'ticking a box' with an EAP counsellor helpline is still more important to HR than actually offering support to prevent serious family disputes arising in the first place due to an essentially toxic family law system. Unfortunately, the fact that much of this support could be provided totally free to employers and employees illustrates a lack of will among HR culturally to offer a much higher level of support, which could measurably improve the company's bottom line. The result of positive initiatives would be a reduction in stress-related absenteeism caused by family break-ups, and a more emotionally intelligent workforce.

Suzy Miller, divorce strategist

Grievance. All employees should have the right to raise a grievance and not be victimised for doing so. Essentially, all feedback is an opportunity to improve situations. For HR, employees are our customers, and as such, we should treat employee grievances as if they are as important as external customer complaints.

Wherever possible, and with full permission from the employee, I always looked to resolve issues informally first. Mostly, I would begin by asking, 'What is your ideal outcome from this situation?'

A SIMPLE SOLUTION

I once had a colleague (whom we'll call Amanda) who raised a grievance about another colleague (we'll call him Bill). Amanda and Bill had been friends for over twenty years. They both worked in the same area, and Amanda's job depended heavily on Bill being supportive, but for some time Bill had been responding aggressively towards her.

Amanda had mentioned Bill's aggression to her managers, but no one had acted on her concerns. She had since been to see her doctor, and she was potentially going to be signed off sick for three weeks with stress.

I interviewed Amanda and Bill separately at first, and Amanda agreed to a later meeting with Bill. I invited both to think about the strengths of their friendship and what they meant to each other.

Bill apologised, explaining that at times he hadn't handled situations well and that he was undergoing counselling due to factors outside of work. In return, Amanda offered to be more supportive. As a result of this open discussion, Amanda came back to work the next day, and Bill implemented some changes in his life to behave in a more professional manner at work.

The director was shocked at how easily we had resolved this issue. I simply explained that at the end of the day, we are all just people, and we all want to be seen, heard and recognised.

All of the grievance meetings I scheduled were arranged as quickly as possible and acknowledged in writing. It can be stressful for employees to be waiting around for an outcome or response to their grievance. Therefore, if I was ever going to be delayed in my investigation, I ensured that I kept them updated with what was going on.

Discipline. In my opinion, disciplinary situations basically mean that, on some level, we in HR haven't engaged, listened to, trained, coached or supported our colleague properly. Some of the managers I have worked with have been too quick to sit someone down and hit them with a warning to punish them for their 'unacceptable' conduct.

Adults behave in a certain way as a result of their mindset. When we discipline them, we are effectively punishing them, which is reactive. Disciplinary situations can be avoided altogether by taking a proactive approach: coaching colleagues to build their mindset through open and honest communication, recognition, appraisals and training. As leaders, we need to look at how we are being.

It is important that each disciplinary situation is handled individually. No two scenarios will ever be the same. Hence, as HR professionals, we must attempt to understand our colleague's point of view and ask what we could possibly have done to prevent the situation from arising. Regardless of the policy, we need to ask if a warning is really the right outcome for the colleague and the business.

In matters of gross misconduct, we should of course follow procedures. However, colleagues must be treated with respect and dignity at all times. Remember that behaviour results from mindset; people act with the level of resources they have available to them. Clearly, I do not condone bad behaviour, but taking some time to understand what is going on in someone's world, causing them to act in the way they have done, shows a level of compassion and understanding that benefits both people and businesses.

The message here is to ensure you follow procedure while treating every individual with dignity and compassion.

A note about warnings. If we effectively carried out all the learnings we gained from leadership training, we probably wouldn't need to issue warnings at all. Warnings do not change behaviour in the long term and, in my experience, they can actually create more issues regarding loyalty. My own view is that we should never be in a situation where we have to issue formal warnings. If we get to this stage, our colleague will almost certainly have decided that their future is not with our company. And if it is, it will not end in a 'happily ever after' scenario. That is why we need to work proactively towards building relationships, engagement and support for our colleagues.

I remember visiting a new client who took me aside to ask a question.

'Where do we stand when one of our staff has requested holiday, but I know she's really going for an interview with another company?'

My response was clear. 'Let's not worry about where we stand, we'll just have an open and honest chat with her.'

From this chat, we learned that the colleague was not attending an interview, but simply taking her son to the hospital as she had said. She did mention that she had applied for other jobs in the past because she had felt overlooked, but she had decided to remain with the company for now. Simply by having this conversation, the client and the colleague were able to clear up any misunderstandings and relieve any concerns.

For me, it's all about understanding what is really going on with a colleague. There is nearly always an underlying issue that is causing them to behave or react in a certain way, so let's be open and brave and get to the root cause, rather than making standard assumptions. This way, we may even be able to help.

Breakdown of trust and values. If you find yourself in a position where there is a complete breakdown of trust and values, and no matter what you do, the employee still feels aggrieved, be brave enough to have an honest conversation about the breakdown. As leaders, we must be responsible for our part in any such breakdown and offer solutions. Unfortunately, one of the solutions may be to part ways, but this still needs to be done with transparency and dignity.

Saying goodbye

> 'Train people well enough so they can leave, treat them well enough so they don't want to.'
> — *Sir Richard Branson*

Exit interviews. These are an extremely useful tool, not just for understanding the reasons why people leave the business, but for the conversations themselves. I often used exit interviews to identify training and coaching opportunities for managers.

Exit interviews are our final opportunity to make a colleague feel valued, to show them that we care and would like them to stay and/or wish them success in their next role. It is important that those leaving the business are treated with respect and dignity throughout the process. There may be a time in the future where they could work with you again or recommend your company to friends and colleagues.

Retirement. Employers in the UK cannot force retirement upon an individual. Over a certain age, workers have the right to retire at any time they choose, and to draw any workplace pension they are entitled to.

From a diversity and inclusion point of view, I feel that older workers bring a wealth of experience and skill to the workplace, not to mention a different outlook to solving problems. I certainly enjoyed the energising mix of ideas generated in staff meetings with older and younger generations working together.

The contributor for this section is another dear friend of mine. Pradip Mistry has worked extensively with various businesses and charities, helping people transition at different stages of their life.

LIFE AFTER WORK

Population changes and workforce ageing are prompting a rethink of retirement by individuals, employers, governments and researchers. Increasing life expectancy and delays in the onset of ill health create potential opportunities for those wanting to perform paid or voluntary work. However, older people will also need to work and save more in the future, given the financial pressures on pensions and public services. The state pension age has been rising to over sixty for women since 2015. To further encourage employment, the government abolished the default retirement age of sixty-five in 2011.

The employer's imperative. The ageing population presents complex challenges to businesses. Many face the prospect of watching their most valuable assets walk out of the door for good when they hit retirement age, taking much of the organisation's knowledge and skill base with them. Businesses will need to develop policies, procedures, and programmes that let their most valuable older workers forge a new kind of connection with the organisation within the framework of a working retirement.

Employers will face the challenge of keeping their organisation fully staffed as the pool of available workers ages. Office for National Statistics data shows that the highest growth in the available workforce over the next ten years will be among fifty-five to sixty-four-year-olds (52%) and among over sixty-five-year-olds (30%). In the same timeframe, employment among thirty-five to forty-four-year-olds will fall by 10%.

Clearly, professional firms have a particular responsibility to help their employees smooth the transition into a working retirement.

Pradip Mistry, transitions coach

Redundancy. Having gone through redundancy myself, I can report that it is an awful experience for anyone, especially people who have been employed with one business for a long time. Although I understood the reasons and the need for my redundancy, the first emotion I experienced was rejection. I was no longer needed, and I wasn't good enough for the business to keep.

After my final redundancy meeting, I had to work a twelve-week notice period. I received little emotional support during these weeks. Gradually, my phone stopped ringing. I stopped receiving emails and I eventually lost contact with my team.

Leaving the business to find a new path was, for me, far more of an emotional challenge than a practical one. However, there was a happy ending to my story. As the saying goes, when one door closes, another one opens. My new door opened to the creation of a career and a lifestyle that I love and am very proud of.

In redundancy situations, we can definitely do more as HR managers. We can offer support, perhaps in the form of helping colleagues update their CV and interview skills. We can keep an open-door policy for colleagues to come and talk about their emotions, and then signpost them to areas of the business or external providers that may be able to support them further.

THE CHALLENGES OF REDUNDANCY

There are a lot of euphemisms for letting employees go – downsizing, outsourcing, rationalisation, organisational change, company review, restructuring and redundancy. Irrespective of whichever labels organisations use, people's emotional reactions tend to be the same.

Of course, there are individuals for whom a redundancy may be welcome. For example, if an individual receives a decent redundancy package, or was unhappy in their work, redundancy offers them an opportunity with financial security to do something else. However, most people do not fall into this category.

Apart from the financial implications, job loss can mean a significant loss of identity and an individual's self-confidence may be eroded. Job loss, like any other form of major loss, can come with many of the emotions akin to bereavement. In addition, a person may feel excluded from society.

Depending on their age, personality type, family and financial circumstances, an individual's reactions may range from mild to severe. The most common reaction to job loss is physical shock, accompanied by some of the classic symptoms associated with grief – disbelief, denial, anger, feeling stunned, becoming withdrawn, loss of confidence, and a feeling of 'why me?' This is particularly true when an individual had no prior warning or sense that they would lose their job.

During a redundancy process, it is likely that your organisation will face the following challenges:

- Employees can feel resentment towards the company and management when they are in a situation where they have limited input, whether such resentment is justified or not

- Any consultation exercise takes time, despite employees commonly wanting an immediate decision. Employees need to be reassured that the employer will make decisions as soon as possible, while ensuring their input is valued and that employment laws are complied with

- It is a stressful time for everyone involved, particularly the employees who will no longer have jobs

- Emotions can run high, which can be followed by acrimony among those affected by the changes

- Redundancies can put your organisation and staff under considerable pressure. Providing external and neutral support can help alleviate such pressure

Pradip Mistry, transitions coach

Dismissal. In matters of gross misconduct, employers should follow timely procedures, with documents presenting evidence and reasons for the colleague's dismissal. Record all meetings, and make sure all representatives and note takers are clear about their role during the meeting.

More importantly – and this is so important that I'm reiterating it here – colleagues must be treated with respect and dignity at all times. Keep all discussions confidential, while ensuring communication with the rest of the team is professional and diplomatic.

We've worked through a lot of detail in the employee cycle step of the Stress-free LEGAL System. Now, let's move on to Step 3.

Step 3: Guides

As a minimum, we must have:

- A contract of employment for every employee

- A handbook that describes the dos and don'ts of the company

- Job descriptions to clarify the roles of each individual

- A guide to company policies (for larger companies)

At best, we in HR need to set up simple systems to ensure our colleagues are well looked after and happy at work. At worst, we need to be able to provide documented evidence to win a case at a tribunal.

Your handbook is a good place to start. A handbook is intended to ensure consistency and clarity, so that everyone is treated fairly. It should provide a clear guide for employees about how things operate in the company and about procedure.

When you're creating a guide, policy or process, make sure it provides the basics:

- Dos and don'ts: how things work
- Flow charts: a step-by-step structure
- Appendices: letters, forms or additional documents to make the system work

Having systems and policies in place ensures that you will have the information in hand when you need it, building credibility as the go-to expert. You will be able to relax in the knowledge that whatever information you need to do your job is easily accessible.

Once you've set up these systems, the team needs to be briefed and trained on how they work. Keep in mind that while you need policies and processes to be in place to clarify expectations and ensure consistency, they will not and cannot define everything about how you manage people.

Step 4: Audits

You can carry out compliance audits annually or periodically, depending on the size of your organisation and how many people are employed there.

You may find HR audits useful to look at:

- Right to work/immigration checks

- Training colleagues have completed

- Appraisals you have completed

- Health and safety

- Holidays colleagues have taken

- Sickness absence process

To help you keep track, create a calendar to map out the completion dates for each audit.

When you're conducting audits, ensure you involve the relevant management team and create action steps together. It is important that you do this with integrity and remain authentic at all times in your partnership with management. Building relationships and respecting the partnership is key. If you work together and engage with others wherever possible, you will create the right environment for compliance.

To make things simple, create easy-to-use templates with relevant questions. Remember that every audit needs a list of action steps to level things up – which brings us on to our final step.

Step 5: Level up

Levelling-up is fundamental to the audit process and ensuring your business is legally compliant. After all, there is no point in working hard to complete an audit if you are not going to take any action. Of course, the action steps are not just your accountability, so yet again, involve management teams and work together to level up successfully.

Book a review date at the beginning of the audit to check that actions have been taken to resolve any exceptions and to sign the actions off properly.

Summary

We've taken a long look at the processes of the Stress-free LEGAL System in this chapter. Before we move on any further, let's recap:

- Ensure that you understand the relevant employment **legislation**. Be proactive, have the right balance between a progress and maintenance mindset, and communicate

- Create policies that encourage a culture of inclusivity and individuality in all three stages of the **employee cycle:** starting, staying and saying goodbye

- Ensure **guides** have clear information that managers and colleagues can be trained on and conversant with

- Conduct **audits** to ensure compliance and record action steps for areas that need to be improved

- Make sure you **level up** and take action to resolve any areas for improvement identified by the audits

CHAPTER FOUR

Productivity

How would your directors and managers feel about the service that you provide if they could see exactly how you add value, and just how well you support the growth of their business? The Winning Results Formula will help you define and measure your productivity, providing you with the tools you need to understand your all-important business goals and check that every role is aligned with achieving them.

In this chapter, we will gain clarity about the people resources you need in your business. We will also discuss the types of reports and information you need to be delivering to directors and managers to demonstrate your progress and value.

There are six steps to the Winning Results Formula:

- Remodel

- Roles

- Requisites

- Results

- Reports

- Resolve

Step 1: Remodel

Once you have a clear idea about what your company wants to achieve, you need to ensure you have resources in exactly the right places to deliver these targets. Organisation charts clarify how the family of the business fits together, helping everybody understand their role and how it connects with the company. This is one of the first things I help my clients with when we begin working together.

Once you have a basic organisation chart, you will then be able to look clearly at your organisation's succession and manpower needs. By forecasting potential changes in your team, you can be proactive, taking steps to recruit as early as possible. Let's face it, delayed recruitment is a pet hate of most managers.

By knowing the people in your business and working closely with managers, you will have a clear idea of what colleagues' intentions are. An honest career discussion with colleagues will help with this process.

Step 2: Roles

'The most helpful job descriptions are living documents that are short and easy to understand, tied to company goals, reviewed regularly by both the colleague and their manager and modified as needed.'
— *Rebecca Mazin and Shawn A Smith*
The HR Answer Book

When you write job descriptions, don't focus on the history of the job. Instead, think about the position as you want it to be, related to the current needs of the organisation. Describe the position itself, and not the individual in the position.

I believe the job description is a key document that enables success for every colleague, including directors and senior managers. I like to include job descriptions in a performance review pack, so every colleague can see exactly what they need to deliver in their job.

Without clear job descriptions, the list of questions that colleagues and managers need answering can be endless. Who conducts appraisals? Who do they go to with issues or concerns? Who would start any disciplinary process? Who deals with customer queries? Who is in charge of maintenance?

I work with clients who are in a period of rapid growth. The operations team needs resources and the HR team doesn't have updated job descriptions. This delays recruitment and creates frustration for the operations team with their increasing workload.

Make sure that you have an updated job description available for every role in your organisation's structure.

Step 3: Requisites

Once you have agreed on a remodel of the organisation's structure and the roles required for the business, you then need to provide the requisites for a highly productive team. To identify what these are you will need to consult the workforce:

- Check whether employees are comfortable – are heating, seating, and noise levels conducive to their wellbeing?

- Ask colleagues if there are any ways of improving their physical environment

- Ensure they have the tools they need to do their job

Step 4: Results

HR is often seen as a function that can't be measured, which I believe is one of the main reasons why many directors and managers do not see its value. But by working closely with the finance team in particular, HR can tangibly support the growth of a business. Helping the directors and managers create some realistic SMART objectives and targets can do a lot to help move a business forward.

SMART stands for: Specific, Measurable, Achievable, Realistic and Time-bound:

- Specific to the area that needs to be improved

- Measurable, so that the outcome is clear

- Achievable, so that what is required is in fact possible

- Realistic, given the resources available

- Time-bound, to be completed by an actual date

A great way to start is by organising a team meeting, ensuring that all business functions are represented. HR can facilitate this meeting, communicating a clear agenda and an ideal outcome. Essentially, it will be a working session that asks the representative of each function to describe the tasks they carry out in their area of the business, considering where they are making losses and where they can potentially make their biggest gains. Based on this information, you can then set targets together for the business, teams and individuals.

Equipped with visible targets, the relevant managers can agree objectives with individual colleagues at their performance reviews, meaning all colleagues should become clear about how they can contribute to the company and its growth.

Step 5: Reports

HR often cannot communicate any tangible results or outcomes. However, there are certain areas within the business in which we can provide informative data about our contribution.

Rather than waiting to be asked for information, how about providing the directors with regular updates on progress and review outcomes from previous meetings? The more understanding and transparency you share with directors and managers, the more you will build a credible and strong working relationship.

In a small business, reports may be created manually, but larger companies may have a dedicated HR information software (HRIS) system in place. I believe that HRIS systems are fantastic, and very cost effective when they're used properly as they save valuable time and paper.

The HRIS system holds data and relevant documentation for all colleagues. It requires you to update information, such as holiday or sickness dates, appraisal dates and forms, regularly. A useful HRIS system needs all managers and HR to work together in ensuring the information is accurate.

However you decide to generate your reports, let's look at some of the information they can provide for the business.

Absence. An absence report provides information on how many hours colleagues are absent each week. Using this data, you can improve payroll costs, improve absence monitoring processes, and consider new options around health and wellbeing for your colleagues.

Holidays. In the UK, all colleagues are entitled to statutory holiday pay. A report on holiday entitlement versus holiday colleagues have taken can help ensure all colleagues receive their annual leave, and that the business does not suffer from the common issue of too many people being away at the same time.

Performance reviews. At best, these should be completed annually, with regular follow-ups. In businesses with fewer than five staff, performance will clearly not need a formal report. However, it is good practice to ensure you keep track of performance reviews.

However small or large your company is, performance reviews are evidence of feedback, objectives you've set, targets colleagues have achieved, career path discussions and training colleagues require, all of which is valuable information that can support an employer's case in a tribunal if needed. I have used this information to create clear plans with my managers, setting achievable targets for completing reviews.

Training. Within every business, there will be a minimum legal requirement of basic training, some of which may include health and safety, fire drills, first aid and/or food hygiene. Such training needs to be tracked, as there could also be a legal requirement for refreshers and retraining. You need to provide this information to the relevant managers to ensure the business is showing due diligence.

Vacancies. If you report on potential resource and succession planning requirements, you could adopt a far more proactive approach to filling vacancies – something directors and managers will appreciate.

Payroll. This is not always down to HR, with payroll often being automated and looked after by the finance team. However, HR is still responsible for making sure that colleagues get paid on time and accurately. Just one negative wage query means we have failed to make a colleague feel valued.

Step 6: Resolve

I was once approached by a colleague who was dissatisfied because she had not been paid all of her overtime in her most recent salary payment. She mentioned that she was going to struggle financially and was disappointed that she would have to wait a whole month before she got paid again. On investigating the issue, I spoke with her manager and the payroll department, and she received her outstanding pay within five days.

When we are doing nothing but firefighting, we can create inaccuracies in our work that affect others. That doesn't mean that we must never make mistakes (we're only human), but we must do whatever it takes to correct the situation.

The easy solution here is not just to provide reports, but to review the data and potential those reports show to make further improvements in the business. In HR, we should not wait for someone to set targets for us. Instead, we look for ways and methods to demonstrate how we can be more efficient, more productive, and add further value to the business.

For example, if sickness levels for the business are reporting at 5%, what can we do to improve this? Do all colleagues and managers understand the procedures? Are the procedures being followed? Are we doing enough to help improve colleague wellbeing? Are there certain colleagues that need further support to attend work? Is there an issue around leadership and loyalty?

If staff turnover is high, what can we do to improve this? What is the business culture like? Are staff having appraisals and regular catch-ups with managers? Are we providing the right working environment? Are we making our colleagues feel valued? What recognition methods do we use? Do our managers have the right leadership skills?

Putting people first and influencing culture

I chose a career in HR because I wanted to influence how employees are treated. For me, this is all about:

- Being a role model and driving collaborative ways of working and teamwork

- Knowing what's going on around me and being able to identify trends and insights within my business area so that people are at the heart of decision making

- Being courageous in challenging others who don't put people first

Let's think about some words and phrases to describe a culture that holds us back:

- Arrogance

- Bureaucracy

- Tell

- Hierarchy

- Process over output

- Killing ideas

- Defensiveness

What does it feel like to work in an environment like this?

Now, let's think about words and phrases to describe the type of culture that takes us forward:

- Trust

- Collaboration

- Listen and learn

- Empowerment

- OK not to have all the answers

- Respect

- Warmth

- Understanding

- Winning together

- Pride

- Innovation

- Resilience

- Drive

- Optimism

- Customer focus

- Risk-taking

- Energy

Which list do you prefer?

HR professionals are the guardians of a company's individual culture, so be brave and make a stand for the colleagues in your organisation. Be great at influencing, having dynamic discussions and making bold requests.

Spend some time reflecting on the culture in your organisation. What one thing can you do now to make a difference?

Here are a few ideas:

- Team events – sharing information and team building activities

- Recognition events – celebrating long service and outstanding performance

- Social events with managers and staff together

- Staff communication sessions

- Introducing a set of core values that are relevant to the business and are easily relatable for everybody

Summary

The purpose of the Winning Results Formula is to support the business in being productive by:

- Reviewing the structure of the organisation, helping to **remodel** and improve clarity of reporting

- Defining job **roles** for each individual in the business by ensuring job descriptions are living documents and a core part of performance review processes

- Providing colleagues with **requisites** to help them do their jobs, ensuring higher productivity. Be concerned about the workplace, give colleagues an opportunity to discuss changes before you implement them, and keep listening out for what colleagues are not saying

- Ensuring there is a growth strategy in place that defines objectives and targets, and everyone knows what they can do to contribute and deliver the **results**

- Updating the business on the contribution you are making towards its growth by providing accurate information **reports**

- **Resolving** to improve on the contribution you make. Take ownership and set your own targets to contribute at a higher level

CHAPTER FIVE

Performance

141

Make your role all about serving your team with what matters most to them, and you will get what matters to you. Performance is a real passion of mine. Without good performance, your business will not grow, and talented people will leave. Good performance means morale will be high and people will be accountable for their contribution towards the growth of your business.

Although this seems simple on the surface, we often get the basics of performance wrong by letting our own opinions and judgements get in the way. Let's begin with the premise that no one comes to work to do a bad job. People generally get into bad habits or behaviours because they are not managed properly – they don't know what their manager expects of them or they are not motivated by their manager. In short, poor performance results from poor leadership.

Managing performance the right way

The old saying goes, 'If we do what we've always done, we'll keep getting what we've always got.' In my experience, the stark reality is that things will, in fact, get worse if they are not continuously improved. Aside from being the name of an old rock band, status quo can result in people becoming bored, less engaged, less productive and, in the end, tempted to leave for greener grass. All this costs a business time, energy, effort and money on recruiting and retraining new team members to replace already well-trained ones. This is bad economics.

So, here's an idea. What if instead of blandly meeting expectations, we exceeded them?

It's far smarter to retain and develop the people we already have in a business than to manage an ineffective revolving door system that constantly forces round pegs into triangular holes. Yet, many companies fail to get this right.

In the past, I very much enjoyed working in teams under effective managers. I gave my all because I knew the manager supported, developed and listened to me properly. They valued me as an individual and wanted the best for me. They encouraged me to grow and achieve my personal goals for a better future. I remember being praised by different managers for the standard of work I delivered, which made me want to achieve even more. Their positive behaviour created loyalty, along with a strong sense of commitment towards them and the business. After all, who wouldn't want to be loyal and committed to a management team like that?

On the flip side, throughout my career I have encountered managers and HR professionals who felt they had to performance manage an employee.

I remember in one of my regional roles, a store manager (let's call her Alison) announced that she was going to take sick leave for stress. Alison had been told in a review meeting that she was going to be performance managed, which had left her feeling nervous and demoralised.

I reviewed her appraisal document together with Alison, and I coached her on how to present herself and her evidence at her next review meeting. More importantly, I coached her on being accountable for her performance. Alison took the feedback on board and became much more self-driven as a result. She received great feedback at her follow-up appraisal review, and she learned how to be more proactive about her performance. This naturally led to improvements.

If you have a colleague who has worked in your business for a while, gathering knowledge and understanding, but who is now underperforming, what is a formal performance management process really going to change? We should never need to threaten a colleague with disciplinary action for poor performance. Aside from the fact that it highlights bad leadership, disciplinary action just doesn't work when it comes to improving performance.

Instead, HR should take a more proactive and supportive role. If we serve our colleagues and genuinely help them find their greatness, we will get far better results compared to dishing out threats of punishment.

Make time to ask your colleagues to explain what's really going on. Remember that our role in HR is to coach and train our managers to be effective and proactive in helping our colleagues perform at higher levels. There is no such thing as poor performance. There is, however, disengagement, and that's down to poor leadership.

> 'You can have everything in life you want, if you will just help other people get what they want.'
> — *Zig Ziglar*

Imagine inviting your colleagues for an open conversation with HR, asking them what their personal goals were at the start of each year and how you could provide support in achieving them. How about following up with meaningful quarterly reviews to make sure you maintain momentum? People would feel more appreciated and significant, knowing that their daily tasks were leading them somewhere rather than nowhere.

Simple tweaks to the way we've always done things can have huge benefits in the long run, with an instant impact on attitudes and results.

An alternative to disciplinary action

Here are some of the things you as an HR profes-sional and / or employer must do before you resort to formal processes:

- Have an informal discussion over a coffee and show genuine interest in what may be on your colleague's mind

- Listen with intent – is there an underlying issue affecting them?

- Let them know you are there to support them

- Establish whether there are any gaps in their training

- Offer coaching and the opportunity to meet regularly for feedback sessions. A great coach always asks the right questions and genuinely wants to help people be better and do better. Help people find their greatness

- Review the colleague's job description with them to set clear expectations

- Agree on SMART objectives so that your colleague has clarity around targets and what success looks like

- Review the colleague's performance – always ensure their managers have conducted fair and consistent documented reviews and follow-ups with honest feedback

In most cases, HR professionals and employers haven't ticked all of these boxes before deciding to performance manage a colleague. Instead, they hope the threat of disciplinary action will magically improve their colleague's performance.

Why not encourage managers to be brave and give honest feedback. You may have seen documented performance reviews that describe a colleague as 'a real asset to the business', when you know that colleague's manager complained to HR about his performance just the week before.

The Born to ACHIEVE Accelerator

Any successful business must develop a people plan that focuses purely on growing people within the business. A good people plan will ensure individuals are in the right place for their skills, so they are free to give their best to the organisation and feel good about doing so.

My Born to ACHIEVE Accelerator model is designed to support the performance of colleagues. It engages them in the business, supporting them to achieve their hopes and aspirations, building realistic action plans, training and coaching them, validating and elevating them.

The ACHIEVE acronym stands for:

- Accountability
- Contribution
- Hopes
- Implement
- Educate
- Validate
- Elevate

Let's take a look at each step.

Step 1: Accountability

Accountability for their performance should sit with each individual. The ultimate 'what good looks like' is that colleagues are seeking out their manager for review meetings themselves, describing what they have achieved and what they are going to deliver.

To implement the accountability process, give your colleagues an appraisal document that includes their job description. Ideally, this document starts with each colleague completing a self-appraisal about their own performance. The outcome of an appraisal should never be a surprise to them. Make sure you have regular discussions with colleagues throughout the year in the form of coffee chats, monthly one-to-one meetings and staff sessions.

The appraisal process only goes wrong when we do nothing, realise our colleagues are not motivated, then threaten to performance manage them. As HR professionals, our role is to ensure that managers are trained on how to conduct effective appraisal meetings, and on the skills that support the performance of their colleagues. If we feel the need to, we can support managers further by sitting in on appraisal meetings and giving detailed feedback.

Step 2: Contribution

Ideally, every employee will be engaged in delivering defined company goals. The business sets these targets and objectives. When people know the contribution they need to make, they connect to their 'why' – why they are doing what they do.

Managers can support their colleagues by developing SMART action plans, which include activities and tasks that everybody can work towards. These need to be designed to motivate colleagues and stretch them to help them grow their potential.

Once you and your colleagues have agreed upon goals, supply them with the training, qualifications and coaching that they may need, and ensure you carry out regular reviews to support progress.

Step 3: Hopes

Everyone has hopes and aspirations. Understanding what makes people tick is important, because as managers, we need to know what really motivates our teams.

Have an open conversation with colleagues about what they want to achieve in their lives over time. Helping them find their 'why' will help them define the reasons they come to work. Ask them what they need from you in terms of support and what training and coaching they may need to achieve their hopes and aspirations. Record their responses on a personal development plan (PDP).

Personal conversations can really help build loyalty between you and your colleague. Make sure you deliver anything you have agreed with them, and plan regular meetings to review progress.

Step 4: Implement

This is the action-taking stage. It can be quite normal for colleagues to become complacent over time and fail to take the actions you agreed on. Regular reviews and support meetings can help managers overcome apathy as they remind each colleague about accountability and achieving their own goals. Often managers are not trained effectively in giving feedback or do not have the necessary coaching skills to help push colleagues forward in their commitments. In HR, our role is to ensure we support those managers and provide them with the necessary skills. Again, you may want to sit in on some of the progress reviews and provide coaching where appropriate.

Step 5: Educate

There will be opportunities for managers and colleagues to achieve qualifications and further skills, provide options and invest in ongoing development. In HR, we are in a position where we can provide a library of courses (or access to one), which will in turn create an environment and culture of continuous learning.

If you have yet to implement this culture of education, create a space in your working environment where colleagues and managers can access information, books, training manuals, online training, and/or the means to book themselves on to relevant courses. Organise development sessions in which colleagues can learn more about management opportunities and growing their potential within the business. This was one of my favourite things to do: sharing my knowledge, inspiring colleagues and managers to bring their greatness to work, and seeing just who they could become.

Step 6: Validate

An appraisal is completely pointless if we don't validate it by following it up and reviewing our colleagues' progress. Follow-ups can be carried out over a cup of coffee while we review appraisal documents and talk openly about progress. Always start with celebrating the colleague's successes, then discuss any challenges they may be facing and agree on further steps. The more regular these follow-up reviews are, the more likely a colleague will be to achieve the goals they relate to.

Step 7: Elevate

When a colleague has achieved the objectives we agreed upon, as a business, we need to show them positive recognition. This could take the form of promotion, a pay raise, or a bonus. Such recognition will elevate our colleagues, motivating them to take on new challenges and grow their potential further.

It's often said that people don't leave jobs, they leave managers. Recognise your talent and be a magnetic manager: someone people will not want to leave.

I hope the Born to ACHIEVE Accelerator model helps you create a team of colleagues who will do just that.

DEVELOPING PEOPLE

Ken Blanchard's book *Situational Leadership II* provides an easy to understand yet complex framework for assessing and aiding the development of an individual. Specifically, it deals with competence and commitment levels.

My experience in leading prior to acquiring this tool was quite painful. In my first leadership role in 2008, my boss was a tough driver, and I had to work closely with my team of ten to please her and keep on top of our workloads. What I learned under the pressures of this role was that my natural instinct or style wasn't always going to work. I found myself spending too much time trying to help people, doing the work myself, not giving proper feedback and being fluffy about what needed to be done.

Situational Leadership taught me to split the development process into two halves: diagnosing and style application. Diagnosing involved working out the coaches' or employees' level of competence and commitment. Then, I set out to apply the right style: one that suited the diagnosed development level.

With zero diagnosis, I got it wrong more than 50% of the time. I created dependencies and lack of clarity among the team as I supported those who needed direction, and directed others who needed coaching – a 'mismatch', according to Blanchard's book. Looking back, I was unstructured and inconsistent in the leadership I was providing.

As leaders, we can't be expected to get it right every time, but being able to place where we went wrong and do it differently next time is what counts. This is what helps us accelerate performance to the next level. It is a must-have tool for anybody in a leadership position who wants to save time and enjoy the fruits of effective delegation.

Ross Trigwell, founder of
The Learning and Development Company

Summary

The purpose of the Born to ACHIEVE Accelerator is to grow and support the potential of our colleagues proactively so that they can contribute to the growth of the business. We do this by:

- Ensuring that our colleagues are **accountable** and take ownership of their performance from day one of their employment journey

- Clarifying the **contribution** that everyone makes to the company goals and targets

- Discussing **hopes** and designing a PDP for the colleague to develop their personal skills and behaviours

- Agreeing on actions and supporting the colleague to **implement** these actions

- Providing a lifelong and continuous learning environment where colleagues can **educate** themselves or access courses to help them expand their skillset

- Following up to check progress. This gives the colleague a sense of **validation** and encouragement. Celebrate along the way and agree on further steps if needed

- **Elevating** our colleagues for their commitment and hard work, giving them recognition for the contribution they have made to the business and for growing as an individual

- Ken Blanchard's *Situational Leadership II* provides an easy to understand yet complex framework for assessing and aiding the development of an individual. Specifically, it deals with competence and commitment levels. By using these tools, we can meet our colleagues' needs rather than hoping they will get it one day and meet our needs in their performance

CHAPTER SIX

Progress

No matter how closely you follow the rest of the advice in this book, without reviewing progress, you will be unclear about your business's expectations, and you will be unable to define future strategy based on tangible results. This leaves room for assumptions and miscommunication. Regularly review progress and you will understand what is expected of you, your team and your business. You will be able to make informed future projections based on actual progress that will identify any changes needed to keep the business growing.

I have devised a handy tool, which I call the Regular Review Routine, to help you review the progress you are making. This tool consists of four key steps:

- Surveys

- Sessions

- Strategy

- Solve

As always, let's look at each step in turn.

Step 1: Surveys

Many large organisations use surveys to find out how their employees feel about working for them. This can be useful in providing a snapshot of a moment in time. The survey is usually conducted online over a set period of time across the whole business.

When I facilitated such surveys in my role as an in-house HR professional, I was required to prepare a briefing for all managers, as well as train them on how to brief their colleagues. We got to work on preparing a wall of great memories to remind our colleagues of the wonderful things the business had provided for them over the previous year. Then, each manager would brief each member of their team and ask them to complete the survey. Once they had completed it, we would use the survey results as a measure of the culture and morale in the business. The HR manager would then review the results with the team and create an action plan, which we communicated and displayed on a wall.

You may be able to tell from the robotic way I've described this process that I personally dislike the routine of conducting a survey to find out how colleagues feel about working in a company. We ask colleagues to complete a survey online, an external company collates the feedback, we wait for the results to come back in the form of a report, then we discuss findings with our colleagues and create action plans. All well and good, isn't it? However, if we are doing everything we are supposed to be doing, namely conducting annual reviews and regular one-to-one meetings, then why do we need to conduct a survey at all? Why not simply talk to our team members, ask them for their opinions and then take immediate action?

Let's involve the whole team in making improvements, sharing accountability and encouraging team spirit. Managers have an important leadership role, with engagement and a shared vision playing their parts, but it is not solely up to management to improve morale; it is the responsibility of everyone who works within the business. Instead of generic surveys, let's have meaningful performance reviews. Let's have one-to-one meetings and be genuinely interested in our colleagues and what goes on in their world. If we are genuinely interested in our colleagues and care about what matters to them, would we need to remind them of the great things the business has done for them? People tend not to forget things that matter to them, after all.

All too often, we use a standard one-size-fits-all approach to measure progress. This makes results generic rather than personal, and we have to work harder to win the loyalty of our colleagues.

Step 2: Sessions

By facilitating structured sessions, you will get the feedback you need to create a strategy for improvement and growth. These include sessions with a group of colleagues, structured meetings with line managers, and a feedback session with key stakeholders.

Staff sessions. Staff sessions – small discussion groups to consider what is going well, what isn't, and what improvements may be helpful – were among my favourite meetings to organise with my colleagues. We carried them out around four times a year, each session involving a selection of colleagues or representatives from each department in the business.

Staff sessions such as these are great opportunities to share new information and communicate changes to colleagues in person. The more we communicate with people face to face, the clearer our message becomes. Not only that, our colleagues will feel valued when we take the time to speak to them rather than sending a generic email from behind our desks.

People have a heartfelt desire to be seen, heard and recognised. Certainly, there were many positive aspects to the simple staff sessions I arranged. They gave colleagues a sense of involvement, which immediately created an open and honest partnership. They also gave employees a sense of responsibility and encouragement because they were part of the decision-making process to grow the business. This in turn created a sense of equal leadership – managers and colleagues making decisions and working together to grow and improve.

The sessions were also great ways to discover talent. I loved hearing the new ideas that colleagues brought forward. It made me smile whenever I recognised potential talent in a colleague; it felt like I was uncovering a gleaming diamond, and it was uplifting to know that with the right coaching and training, these colleagues could become leaders of the future.

Structured meetings. I was amazed whenever I heard stories of poor team relationships, whether with a direct manager or with teams that worked in the business, from my HR peer group. For me, the best way to resolve any issue is to talk. If we go back to the simple notion of HR providing an essential business service, by not being open and honest, we are failing to offer the very service we have signed up to deliver.

HR exists to enable the growth of a business and its people. This means that we need to be bigger than ourselves and stay focused on the business's vision. We are often the key influencers of managers and directors, who need to feel properly supported.

Regular structured meetings, with a formal agenda, will help keep the communication flowing. I often lead and facilitate such meetings, and I am regularly the person who will ask open questions that address any elephants in the room head on. We should never be afraid to speak the truth, as long as the truth can be appropriately backed up with data. While this can be challenging, the Dynamic Discussion model that we met in Chapter 2 will help when we're relaying or communicating difficult messages.

My commitment to proactive HR means that I plan structured meetings well in advance, communicate with the relevant attendees, and provide a clear purpose and agenda for the meeting. No one wants to sit in meetings that have been arranged just for the sake of it, going round in circles with no direction and not achieving anything. We need to be better than this, because we won't build any credibility by wasting everybody's time.

Feedback sessions with key stakeholders. As an HR professional, I spent 80% of my time with people – directors, managers, colleagues or associates. Scheduled and structured meetings ensured we enjoyed open communication, strong accountability and solid relationship building. To help with the smooth flow of a discussion and information, I ensured I targeted my communications accordingly.

With directors, the emphasis was on reviewing the business goals and progress, along with clear targets. With managers, the discussion was about reviewing their progress with their goals and objectives after their performance review, detailing any support they required and how they were feeling in general about their job, health and family. With associates, the conversation was centred on reviewing our relationship – what worked, what needed improving, sharing experiences of best practice and any new insights we could benefit from. With colleagues, the discussion involved a staff session to discover what was going well, or what we might need to improve. I would also schedule time to speak to colleagues at their work stations, finding out how their day was going and checking that they had received the latest company communication.

Occasionally, managers and colleagues wanted to speak to me about something urgent or on an ad-hoc basis, and I made sure that my schedule was flexible enough to accommodate this. While it wasn't always immediately possible in non-urgent cases, I would schedule a meeting and ensure I followed up on everything.

Step 3: Strategy

It is a given that every meeting you organise must involve a clear outcome and a record of the next steps you and your colleague agree upon – what needs to be done, who will do it, and when they will do it by. These next steps form part of the strategy for improvement and growth of the business.

Generally, the areas of improvement will link to one of the five areas of the HR Brand Blueprint – partnership, process, productivity, performance and progress. Once you have collated all the feedback from your meetings, hold a strategy session with the managers/directors to identify solutions. Celebrate and share the feedback and the plan with everyone who took part in the sessions so that they can see the value of attending and the contribution they made. Involve them as much as possible in completing the action plans.

Step 4: Solve

As a credible HR professional who provides a service and who represents the HR brand, you must follow through on your promises and be accountable for the growth of the people within the business, and also for yourself. It's all well and good having great plans, but they are of no value if you just leave them in a folder on a shelf. You need to highlight and solve any concerns or issues. Plans, if you review them regularly with the team, will be a live working document.

Communicate well and keep people updated with the progress of action plans.

Summary

The purpose of the Regular Review Routine is to ensure that we measure progress within the business. We are often great at the planning and the doing, but it is all too easy to forget the review. This tool allows us to keep being open and honest by drawing a line in the sand and giving us the option to ask, 'What next? How can we further improve our business and take it to the next level?'

- **Surveys** are not my favourite tool to measure culture and morale, but they can provide a snapshot of information at a given time

- **Sessions** are brilliant for instilling a sense of engagement. Asking open questions and listening to the ideas and views of our colleagues will not only make them feel that their opinion is valued, but also give us a chance to spot potential talent and find future leaders to develop

- Once we have collated all the feedback, we need to hold a **strategy** session with the managers/ directors to identify solutions

- Any concerns or issues must be highlighted and **solved**

Conclusion

As we come to the end of this book, I have a confession to make. When I conducted my research, which involved asking HR professionals what they would like to learn more about, the majority told me they wanted to understand employment law, managing poor performance and how to handle difficult situations. But if I'm going to be authentic and true to what I believe, I have to confess that employment law is secondary to engagement and leadership.

As if I needed any more convincing that I was on the right track with this book, I recently attended a prominent workshop that detailed how to investigate facts for a disciplinary meeting. Throughout the session, the conversation kept returning to one simple fact: if we engage, train and coach our people properly, we won't need to worry so much about the law. Overall, I'm pleased that I stuck to my own instincts and believed in myself. I take pride in the fact that the HR Brand Blueprint is all about how we behave as HR professionals and about taking a more balanced approach than that offered by the law alone.

The HR Brand Blueprint will support you as an HR professional in any company that you choose to work with. It will also help you grow as an individual while you develop your career. Living the brand, as I've described in this book, will help you to feel more at peace in your role because it is very much about being proactive.

I only work with clients who are prepared to commit to a long-term relationship, because when I have an understanding of how they work, what they do and what's important to them, I can be proactive in the support I give them. We create something together.

Let's summarise the HR Brand Blueprint and how it can be applied in everyday living.

The HR Brand Blueprint Scorecard

Partnership is at the core of everything we do. Use the Dream TEAM Template to:

- **Tune in.** Be curious about the business and its people. What are the challenges? Who are the customers? What is the bottom line result the company is aiming for and how can you support it?

- **Engage.** Model servant-leadership and put your people first. Be open to using your emotional intelligence to sense your own impact on others. Regularly check in with how leaders, managers and employees are really feeling. What do you know about them and what matters to them?

- **Associate.** Develop your team and network to create solid, collaborative relationships with strong people who have your back. Who is on your team?

- Develop your **mindset.** Build your skills every day. Make a list of the work you have done around your personal development and a brief plan of what you are going to do.

Know your **processes**. Use the Stress-free LEGAL System to be the expert in:

- **Law.** Keep up to date with changes in the law, refresh your knowledge and keep everyone informed on any potential impact. Are there any employment law updates happening in your area?

- **Employee cycle.** Treat colleagues like VIPs when they start, while they stay with your business and when they say goodbye. Do you have clear processes in place for each of these areas?

- **Guides.** Set up guides containing dos and don'ts, flow charts and appendices to ensure consistency, so that when things do go wrong, colleagues have a clear process to follow. Are the necessary guides available when you or your colleagues need them?

- **Audits.** Agree on how you will ensure the business is compliant with the law and complete regular audits. What audits have you completed recently?

- **Levelling-up.** Make sure you take action and are compliant, both with legislation and your own policies. Do you have clear action plans and do you use them as working documents?

We use the six steps of the Winning Results Formula to measure our **productivity** – our contribution to the business – and to provide relevant feedback.

- **Remodel.** A structure and a clear hierarchy will avoid confusion and clarify who does what in the business. Is there an up-to-date organisational structure in place in your business?

- **Roles.** Develop a clear job description for every position on the organisation's structure chart

- **Requisites.** Have you provided the basics for employees to be comfortable? Is there a win-win-win culture in place? What is the morale like within the business?

- **Results.** What you do needs to be aligned with the company goals, such as growth, costs and return on investment. What are the KPIs within your business?

- **Reports.** Provide appropriate reports and updates to managers, leaders and directors. What reports are you providing the business with and how frequently?

- **Resolve.** Follow up on any discrepancies and missing results. What areas can you improve performance in?

Use the Born to ACHIEVE Accelerator to develop **high performance** within your team. Look at:

- **Accountability.** The employee and not the manager should be accountable for their performance. HR can help clarify responsibilities and give employees the freedom to take the lead in their performance. Are your employees accountable for their own performance?

- **Contribution.** Align goals with objectives, so that employees and managers can clearly see how they are contributing towards the company's growth. Are your company goals aligned with employee objectives?

- **Hopes.** Make time to understand what matters to your employees. What are their hopes and aspirations? How can you help bring them to life?

- **Implement.** Execute SMART action plans to deliver objectives, hopes and aspirations.

- **Educate.** Provide regular and relevant training and courses to refresh colleagues' knowledge and develop their skills. What courses and training programmes are available for your staff?

- **Validate.** Follow up and check progress on a regular basis.

- **Elevate.** Recognise and reward achievements and celebrate success. What recognition methods do you have in place?

Use the Regular Review Routine to obtain feedback on colleagues' **progress** and keep the business constantly moving forward. The steps of this tool are:

- **Surveys.** Is your business ready to complete a staff survey, and are you in a position to take action depending on the results?

- **Sessions.** Arrange group meetings with selected staff and managers/directors to identify what improvements you can make and what's going well

- **Strategy.** Create an action plan and encourage employees to take on individual tasks that will help bring improvements; plan for separate meeting times with your directors, managers, line managers and employees to review progress

- **Solve.** A plan is useless unless you make sure you and your colleagues take action to solve any issues you have pinpointed

If you do all this well, then you will be living in the zone of the HR Brand Blueprint and putting the human back into HR.

References And Further Resources

Armstrong, S and Mitchell, B (2008) *The Essential HR Handbook*. Newburyport, MA: Career Press.

Carnegie, D (2017) *How to Win Friends and Influence People* (e-book). Musaicum Books.

Covey, S R (1999) *The 7 Habits of Highly Effective People*. New York: Simon and Schuster.

Fisher, N I (2013) *Analytics for Leaders: A Performance Measurement System for Business Success*. Cambridge: Cambridge University Press.

Mitchell, B and Gamlem, C (2017) *The Big Book of HR*. Newburyport, MA: New Page Books.

Pattni, D (2017) *Recruitment Gems Uncovered: The Ultimate Guide to Guaranteed Success & Wealth in Your Industry*. CreateSpace.

Smith, S and Mazin, R (2011). *The HR Answer Book: An Indispensable Guide for Managers and Human Resources Professionals*. Nashville, TN: Amacom.

Practical support

For further support in your development and career, my Practical HR Skills workshop will help you make the lessons in this book come to life. You can find further information at www.hrtrainingandconsulting.com/hracademy

Online resources

Suzy Miller: www.startingovershow.com
Pradip Mistry: www.lifesmistry.co.uk
Kalpesh Patel: www.thekalpeshpatel.com
Deenita Pattni: www.viamii.com
Ross Trigwell: www.thelearninganddevelopmentcompany.co.uk

Acknowledgements

I want to thank all the people who have supported, guided and inspired me to reach this point.

I will start by acknowledging my family: my mum, my stepdad, my dad and my stepmum for their support and unconditional love; my brothers Jit, Chandz and Aanand for their amazing encouragement and for being my heroes; my sister Vips, who continues to support me with her love and PA duties to keep me on track; my sisters-in-law Champa, Versha and Bhavina for their love and support; and my niece, Diya, and nephews, Adi and Yash, for their beautiful smiles and endless hugs.

Thanks to Pia's dad, Hetan, for being the amazing father he is to her and supporting me unconditionally, and to my mother-in-law, Lina, for making sure I was eating well while working long hours through the early stages of my business.

Janette Jones, my coach, thank you for believing in me when I didn't believe in myself. You were more than a coach; you never gave up on me even when I wanted to give up on my goals: checking in on me when I didn't expect you to, you wanted success for me more than I did in my doubtful moments and you gave your all to make sure I made it happen.

Cheryl Chapman, my ACE coach, thank you for making this more than a job, giving me 100% of yourself during my sessions, and helping me create my system, write my story, and believe that what I have created is necessary.

Kalpesh Patel, an enlightened entrepreneur and life mentor, thank you for giving me access to the most amazing gift of personal development in the form of the Landmark Education, which allowed me to grow in to my possibility. You held a graceful space of love and emptiness so that I could find my own answers; you taught me that things happen when they do, in their own time.

Baiju Solanki, my business mentor, thank you for teaching me to lean in to challenges and take on what is uncomfortable. You created a sense of safety during the most difficult times.

Thank you to my HR mentors who, over the years, have inspired and motivated me to operate to high standards, specifically Marne Cheeseman, who taught me the importance of knowing my stuff, and Sarah King, who taught me how to be human in HR.

Thank you to my managers and directors: Ken Towle for seeing the talent in me, taking a chance and developing me to reach senior management level; Keith Price for showing me that I am significant and how easy it is to make people feel important at work; Sean Dunlea for always valuing my opinion, taking me with him and showing me the power of loyalty; John Cruikshank for teaching me to take the lead and stay true to my plan; and Newall Stratten for inspiring me to be true to my personal brand of being passionate about people.

A heartfelt thank you to the peers who have become my extended family: Lucky Kaur, Dan Weintrob, Denise Peart, Karen Robinson-Fiagbe and Martin Brimicombe. You have always believed in me, stayed with me and supported my efforts to stand out from the crowd. Louise Berry and John Spafford, my colleagues and friends who stayed loyal and kept me going after our redundancies, thank you for your time, patience and feedback on this book.

To Nina Jervis, thank you for taking my words and adding your magic to them to create a unique masterpiece.

My book coach, author Michelle Watson, thank you for guiding me through the final stages of the book. Your support, encouragement and patience pushed me to get over the wall.

Thank you to my friends and contributors who provided their expertise and support – Deenita Pattni, Denise Peart, Suzy Miller, Ross Trigwell, Pradip Mistry and Kalpesh Patel. You have spiced up this book with your truths.

The last and most heartfelt thank you goes to all the people who continue to allow me to mentor and coach them, and who give me the biggest thrill of my career. Seeing you grow and persevere to achieve your goals is rewarding beyond words and makes me want to do more than I already do.

The Author

Su Patel is the founder and director of HR Training and Consulting Ltd. She started her career in 1988 with one of the biggest retailers in the UK, and after twenty-seven successful years she took a redundancy package. She decided to share her experience with a wider au- dience, creating a company to  transform HR in small and medium-sized enterprises (SMEs), and to train and empower HR professionals globally to provide a world-class, human-centred ap- proach to the profession.

Su is passionate about people development and has made it her personal mission to support SMEs as they rarely have access to the right information. They of- ten get caught out because they simply do not know what they do not know!

Su also understands that working in HR can be quite challenging. Finding the right balance between what the business needs and doing the right thing for employees is no easy task for a HR professional, and it often creates an environment of overwhelm and poor decisions.

Her training and coaching programmes are designed to focus on the practical and people-focused reality of working in HR on a daily basis, so that HR professionals can develop a rounded and well-regarded function to partner their business.

'As leaders we have a duty of care to our employees, to help them develop and achieve their personal goals. If we want to keep great talent, we must become servant-leaders – which means we must listen to them and proactively help them grow. There is nothing complicated about people management – after all, we are all just people. Once we understand what's important for one another we can serve one another better.'

Thank you for joining me on this journey, and I wish you every success in your HR career.

For further information about the services I can provide, please visit www.hrtrainingandconsulting.com

Social media

LinkedIn: www.linkedin.com/in/su-patel-mcipd-a3093ba2
Facebook: www.facebook.com/su.patel.73
YouTube: www.youtube.com/channel/UCKwihl3P5Qa0E_Q1X3gC_ww

Printed in Great Britain
by Amazon

86248487R00112